Crime Control

The Use and Misuse of Police Resources

CRIMINAL JUSTICE AND PUBLIC SAFETY

Series Editor: Philip John Stead
John Jay College of Criminal Justice
The City University of New York
New York, New York

FEAR OF FEAR: A Survey of Terrorist Operations and Controls
in Open Societies
John B. Wolf

CRIME CONTROL: The Use and Misuse of Police Resources
David John Farmer

Crime Control

The Use and Misuse of Police Resources

David John Farmer

Virginia Commonwealth University
Richmond, Virginia

Plenum Press • New York and London

Library of Congress Cataloging in Publication Data

Farmer, David John, 1935–
   Crime control.

   (Criminal justice and public safety)
   Bibliography: p.
   Includes index.
   1. Police administration—United States. I. Title. II. Series.
HV8141.F37   1984   351.74′0973   84-11470
ISBN 0-306-41688-3

351.74
F234c

86-734

© 1984 Plenum Press, New York
A Division of Plenum Publishing Corporation
233 Spring Street, New York, N.Y. 10013

Printed in the United States of America

To Rory
and to
Damien, Mark, Gregory, and Elizabeth

Foreword

The question of how to use police resources productively, particularly in this era of tight municipal budgets, is a major concern for police chiefs and others responsible for crime control. In *Crime Control: The Use and Misuse of Police Resources,* David J. Farmer provides new insights into this question and suggests a practical resource allocation approach for police policymakers and administrators. The book documents the results of current police resource allocation practices and describes the major research studies that have identified a need to restructure police field operations. It very usefully outlines the development and nature of allocation techniques and analyzes the political contexts which influence resource allocation. After describing planning at the neighborhood level that should inform the allocation process, the author provides a comprehensive "planning-budgeting-resources allocation" approach to managing a productive police department.

This comprehensive approach is illustrated by an account of the Manpower Allocation Review System (MARS), which the author developed and introduced in the New York City Police Department in 1972 when I was commissioner. As I can attest, the MARS approach had practical utility. For the author, it served as a forerunner to the more elaborate system he describes in this book.

In recent years, American policing has benefited greatly from the observations and analyses of scholars and researchers, particularly when they have had on-line experience in police agencies at one or another stage in their careers. David J. Farmer is a scholar who has had such experience, which adds a special dimension to his observations and conclusions.

Patrick V. Murphy

Preface

How can crime be controlled more effectively? The wide-spread public urge for an easy answer to this difficult question reflects not only the seriousness of the problem but also a general reluctance to treat the matter as seriously as it deserves. Despite fluctuations in the crime data and despite improvements in criminal justice operating practices over the past decade and a half, we remain denied the fullest benefits of urban and other living by the grossness and the extent of our most crippling social disease—crime. Despite the real gains in understanding about criminal justice, public policymaking and debate about crime control remain shackled by dualistic thinking and by the child-like impulse for simplistic answers. The dualistic character of the thinking, assuming only a dichotomous world of "right versus wrong" and "we versus they," is reflected in the nature of our perennial debates over gun control and capital punishment. The urge for the "one-liner" solution is reflected in the character of the remedies commonly touted for the crime problem—"Lock them up and throw away the key;" and "Abolish unemployment;" and "Eliminate the insanity defense." As long as we are constrained by a proclivity toward such instant solutions, we will remain impotent in addressing the crime control problem.

This book presents an analysis and a policy agenda that focus on a subject critical for crime control—the use and misuse of police resources. First, it is concerned with police resources allocation decision-making. It describes present practices and techniques, provides new information on these approaches, and then presents a new framework for understanding and developing allocation techniques. Second, it describes the critical features of a new form of police agency that is required if police resources are to be used effectively and if society is to reduce the crime problem. It outlines the nature of the new form and specifies the policy steps required for implementation. The analysis, while straightforward, does require reconsideration of traditional and comfortable conceptions. It describes the necessity for a reconceptualization of the utilization of police resources, both in the nature of police resources allocation decision-making and in the very form of the police agency. The policy agenda, while offering a potent and needed approach for crime control, is no "hair tonic" remedy. Rather, it presents an effective framework which, with much additional effort, can assure over time that the crime control problem will be addressed to permit the quality of living to which we aspire.

This analysis and policy agenda are based on an interdisciplinary information base. Research data have been collected and analyzed from a survey of United States cities with populations over 100,000, from a survey in a selected state of communities with populations over 5,000, and from participant observation case studies. The techniques and concepts of microeconomics have been applied to the analysis of resources allocation decision-making, and reliance is placed on criminal justice research and other literature. The views expressed have also been shaped by the writer's own experiences—for example, as Special Assistant to the Police Commissioner in the New York City Police Department, and as Director of the Police Division of the National Institute of Justice at the U.S.

Department of Justice. The analysis and policy agenda represent an amalgam of analysis, synthesis, and research.

At one level, this book—it is explained in Chapter 1—is a twin institutional "biography." It analyzes police resources allocation decision-making; and it also offers an analysis of the total police institution by means of its account of a "new form of police agency." At another level, Chapter 1 explains that the book is a call to arms. It is such because of three contentions. First, crime can, and needs to be, more effectively controlled. Second, police resources can be more effectively used, and they must be better utilized if the crime control problem is to be addressed. Third, only by pursuing a policy agenda that works toward a new form of police agency can this more effective utilization be realized.

Concerning resources allocation decision-making, this book documents results indicating the opportunity for the better utilization of police resources and suggesting the shape of the fundamental changes needed throughout the entire range of police operational practices. It describes the development and character of the major types of resources allocation techniques, and presents survey information showing that the police resources allocation decision-making process is more complex in critical respects than the criminal justice literature implies. It demonstrates and illustrates the political context of allocation decision-making, and argues for a reconceptualization of the resources allocation process that considers the political and other factors underlying the decision-making. It presents a conditional model of police resources allocation decision-making. This model shows that conditions determine the extent to which resource allocation decisions are politicized, and it suggests the possibility of controlling or manipulating these conditions. The conditional model presents police policymakers and managers with the prospect that they need not be merely the victims of political influence. The book presents a socioeconomic view of the purpose of policing that supplements the descriptions already in the literature, and it emphasizes how neighborhood-level and realistic planning must be part of the resources allocation process. It offers a new perspective on the allocation process, using the vantage point of economics literature. It specifies a comprehensive "planning-budgeting-resources allocation" approach that can form a practical and sound basis for improving resources allocation decision-making and results, and it illustrates aspects of this approach by describing a system developed by the author for application in the New York City Police Department. The book provides comments on the policy beginnings required of police managers and elected officials wishing to improve resource allocation practices.

Concerning the police institution, the book documents how the contemporary police institution is less than adequate in meeting society's needs. It describes and illustrates how the police institution is afflicted by a dedication to process that should be displaced by greater emphasis on purpose. It observes how, turned inward, the contemporary police institution is suffering from deep bureaucratic malaise that can be broken only by opening lines for an effective working relationship between the political and the programmatic. Needed is a new form of police institution that is open to the extent that the contemporary institution is closed. This new purpose-oriented and accountable form, proceeding beyond the professional model, requires effective political involvement. This new form can address the three realities of police political relations. It must accept that politics permeates policing; that police decision-making can be improved not by denying but by recognizing and manipulating the political element; and that, while some are bad, certain political intrusions are necessary and desirable for fully effective performance. The policy leadership role of the community, acting through its elected officials, is described as critical for establishing the purposive, open type of police institution that is necessary if crime is to be adequately controlled. Reliance on the politician is noted as necessary in establishing the "profit-making burden" on the police administrator and in insisting on police receptivity to new modes of thinking. The book notes how

politicians are failing in their management of the police function, and suggests practical policy beginnings for better
results.

The new form of police agency that is needed for effective
crime control is described as one structured, staffed, and managed so that it has two major capabilities beyond the professional model. Possession of these capabilities, acting synergistically with a third which is part of the professional model,
would ensure evolution of the police institution into the
required new form. The professional model is described as
one which has dominated the modern development of policing and where the drive for operating effectiveness/efficiency
is based on professional autonomy, professional knowledge,
and the service ideal. The first characteristic of the new form
of police agency is the capacity for developing—in partnership with other public and private agencies—workable purposes, plans, and policies for realizing higher levels of order,
law, and justice in the community. The second is the capacity
for mobilizing and leading agencies and individuals in order
to achieve order enhancement, with an emphasis on working
not only directly but also indirectly through other societal
organizations. The third, a feature of the professional model,
is the capacity for utilizing research results and new perspectives as much as possible in agency thinking about its "doing"
activities—the capacity for being creative. The book describes
the relevance for crime control of this new form of police
institution that is purpose-oriented, outgoing to the environment, and creative.

The basic policies or approaches described do constitute a
genuine policy agenda for communities wanting effective
crime control. It is explained that the term "policy" is used
throughout to emphasize the need to concentrate on the fundamental arrangements for allocating resources and for establishing the new form—the need to focus on the basic arrangements of the new form before addressing the nitty-gritty
administrative difficulties attendant on any fundamental
change. While the thrust of the book is away from the preva-

lent but unrealistic "criminal justice impulse" for instant results, advice is added for managers and politicians wishing to make policy beginnings toward the more effective utilization of their resources.

This book has been written for two main reasons. The first is that, while the literature on aspects of these topics is extensive, it has been possible to break new ground in this book in developing our understanding of the utilization of police resources. We will leave to the reader's generosity to judge whether this book, as it claims, has made significant contributions to advancing knowledge concerning the techniques and practice of using police resources. The second reason is that this study convinces the author that the pessimistic view so common about crime control is unrealistic. This pessimism considers that little can really be done to cope with the crime situation. On the contrary, this book shows that the new form of police agency can give us the beginning we want in addressing our crime problems, and it indicates that we have the capability and the information to begin effecting these needed changes now. We can overcome. We can enjoy the minimal crime hazards and the higher caliber of policing that we deserve.

Virginia Commonwealth University
Richmond, Virginia

D.J.F.

Acknowledgments

In writing any serious book on criminal justice and police issues, the primary debt that must be acknowledged is to the practitioners and researchers who made it possible. Over the years, the author has been fortunate to receive guidance, information, and example from many excellent police commanders in departments throughout the country—and from some poor ones. The debt to the many criminal justice researchers and thinkers is equally clear from the text. This book stands on their shoulders.

In this vein, particular acknowledgment is made to the contribution of former colleagues and associates in Public Administration Service, the Jacobs Company (Planning Research Corporation), the New York City Police Department, and the National Institution of Justice in the U.S. Department of Justice. It is also owed to my present colleagues on the faculty of the Department of Administration of Justice and Public Safety at Virginia Commonwealth University.

Special thanks for his help are extended to my editor and friend, Philip John Stead, former Dean of Graduate Studies at the John Jay College of Criminal Justice and former Academic Dean of the Police Staff College, Bramshill. Thanks also to col-

leagues who offered comments on the draft—Paul W. Keve,
former director of the state correctional systems in Minnesota
and Delaware; David Geary, former police chief of Ventura
and other departments; Michael McDonald, Director of our
Department's Transportation Safety Training Center; and to
Rosemary Lee Farmer, Associate Director of Family and Children's Service of Richmond. Responsibility for errors of fact
and opinion, of course, remain with the author.

Thanks to the editor of *Police Studies* for permission to use
and adapt materials from two articles written by the author in
that magazine. The articles are entitled "Thinking About
Research: The Contribution of Social Science Research to Contemporary Policing" (Vol. 3, No. 4, Winter 1981), and "Police
Resources Allocation: Toward a Theory" (Vol. 5, No. 2, Summer 1982).

Particular thanks are due also to my secretary, Gloria E.
Washington, for her heroic efforts in typing and retyping this
manuscript.

This book is dedicated to my wife Rory, my companion
in all things, and to my children, Damien, Mark, Gregory, and
Elizabeth. My hope is that this book will make a contribution,
however small, toward rendering police policymaking and
management safer for them—and for America.

Contents

Crime and Police Resources: A Policy Agenda

Crime can be effectively controlled to the extent that communities make more appropriate use of their police resources, and this control can be achieved without abrogating civil liberties and without inordinate financial cost. Needed is a new form of police agency. Without a policy agenda for working toward such a new form, communities will continue to misuse—to misallocate—their police resources; without the reallocation made possible by such a new form, crime will remain inadequately controlled. Such a new form is feasible. In the course of examining the problems of police resources allocation, this book specifies the shape of such an agency and outlines what can be done to create the new form.

Needed, in other words, are new understandings and improved practice in the utilization of police resources. The use and misuse of police resources—or police resources allocation—is a vitally important issue for crime control, as it is for police policy-making and management. What is police resources allocation? At this point, let us note only that police resources allocation is a larger subject than it is commonly taken to be. It is characterized—inappropriately—in the criminal justice literature as the narrow, technical problem of deploying manpower (and womanpower)[1] among alternative geographical uses and among functional activities. How many officers should be assigned to one precinct rather than to another, for example? Viewed from one end of the telescope, police resources allocation is indeed the narrow and merely technical matter of determining how many employees shall do what, where, when, and how—a concern for bureaucrats. Viewed from the other end of that telescope, however, resources allocation decision-making is a fundamental issue of crime control policy-making and politics—determining which citizens shall get what, where, when, and how. How many officers, for example, should be assigned to the central city, to the suburbs, to the ghetto, to the affluent sector? How many should be allocated to preventing violent crime, to investigating street crime, to convicting organized crime racketeers, . . . to issuing parking tickets?

First, crime can, and needs to be, more effectively controlled. Second, police resources can be more effectively used, and they must be better utilized if the crime control problem is to be addressed. Third, only by pursuing a policy agenda that works toward a new form of police agency can this more effective utilization be realized. As beginning points, then, let us address in turn aspects of these contentions—of the crime control problem, of the resources allocation dilemma, and of the nature of the new form of police agency.

The new form is described, under the subheading "New Form of Police Agency," toward the end of this first chapter. Following that, we will be in a better position to indicate the character and contents of this book. Its character will be seen as an amalgam of analysis, empirical research, and synthesis

---

[1] Henceforth, let us assume that masculine words also include the feminine.

conducted over a twelve-year period. The contents will be viewed as providing new perspectives on a much misunderstood topic that is central to effective crime control—the use and misuse of police resources. The significance, it is hoped, for practical improvement will be appreciated by the wide spectrum of audiences being addressed—by practitioners, academics and students of criminal justice, by public sector policy-makers, elected officials and professional administrators, and by all who care about America's "number one" domestic problem.

BEGINNING POINTS

As a topic of serious study criminal justice has enjoyed quantum growth in recent years, largely resulting from the huge (and unhappily truncated) investment of the Federal Government in efforts to improve criminal justice. Criminology has of course been a scholarly subject for a much longer time. The volume of research available on criminal justice issues is now truly gargantuan, and schools and departments of criminal justice flourish throughout the country. The quality of such research has grown no less significantly. There does exist, in brief, a substantial and important body of knowledge on criminal justice. Unfortunately, many persons in newspaper offices as well as in barrooms still believe that criminal justice is really little more than a matter of opinion. Combined with the reality that criminal justice issues raise deep emotions and are bedevilled by a rich variety of myths and misunderstandings, this outlook makes the discussion difficult. The discussion is especially tense when addressing such sensitive issues as crime control, utilization of police, and change required in the character of police service—the present topics for preliminary consideration. Paragraphs on criminal justice do seem to move the adrenal glands.

Crime Control

Crime control, as a topic of conversation, is blessed with
an extensive literature and cursed by a multitude of unan-
swered questions. Among the available answers, the following two are critical. First, the causes of crime and criminality
are multitudinous and multilayered. They can be economic,
social, psychological, political, institutional, biological ... ;
others will suggest additional categories such as the character
of the legal code or aspects of historical development. Not
only is there no one cause of crime and criminality but also
crime itself is not a unitary phenomenon. By this it is meant
that there are many different kinds of crime and criminals,
and each kind may result from a different set of causes. These
causes are multilayered in that they have varying degrees of
immediacy relative to the crime or criminal. What caused the
teenager to commit a particular daytime burglary? The act
may have resulted from any number of underlying factors—
his diet, for example. But a variety of intermediate factors
must be expected, e.g., the school's truancy program.

Second, there is no panacea, no quick-fix, for the crime
problem. The error of the Great Society programs, of which
crime control was one, was an underlying thesis that the
quick-fix is possible. "America can control crime, if it will,"
concluded the President's Commission on Law Enforcement
and Administration of Justice (President's Commission, 1967);
and a succession of LEAA administrators were then compelled
to develop and administer crime control programs under the
gun of the quick-fix expectation. This expectation that there
must be a simple, immediate solution plagues most public discussion of the crime control problem, and frustrates specification of appropriate public policy. This quick-fix approach to
crime control is particularly evident in some attitudes toward
civil liberties, as some focus on particular features of the legal
system such as the insanity plea or the activity of the U.S.
Supreme Court. Certainly, curtailment of civil liberties can be
utilized for crime control purposes, as declarations of martial

law attest. Certainly, the exercise of some civil liberties at some times can result in the guilty going free. And certainly, some amount—it is hoped, a modicum—of crime may be the inevitable price of the maintenance of civil liberties, as the "grease is necessary for the wheel."

These two considerations about crime control have clear implications for this study. First, our study is concerned only with one aspect of crime control—the range of service that can be obtained through a police agency. Thus, much that is fundamental is omitted. But, as is indicated in the later descriptions, the new form of police agency is one that would play a much larger, and more significant, part in planning and action programs concerning the whole range of crime causation factors; it is seen here as a mechanism for developing, administering, and coordinating community policy with regard to all these factors. Second, this book does not pretend to offer a panacea. Effective crime control is a complex, difficult, and long-range matter. What the present study does is to offer a sensible framework which—with much effort, frustration, and commitment of talent—can assure over time that the crime control problem will be addressed. But it offers neither a simple nor an immediate solution; that much is impossible.

An assumption underlying these comments is that we do indeed have a "crime problem" to be controlled, which thus raises two questions. How do we know about, and how do we measure, crime in the United States? What is the extent of the crime problem in the United States? The answers are relatively straightforward. First, the two sources of information for measuring crime in the United States are police agencies and crime victims. Police have gathered crime statistics for more than fifty years under the Uniform Crime Reports program, now administered by the Federal Bureau of Investigation; more than 15,000 police agencies, covering some 98 percent of the population, participate in this voluntary program. Crime statistics from crime victims are collected through the National Crime Survey conducted by the Bureau of the Census on behalf of the U.S. Department of Justice.

Both data sets have well-established and marked limitations. The former is dependent on the reliability of reporting
agencies, for example, and this reliability is limited to the
extent that a number of local agencies practice data manipulation and downgrading of incidents from one crime category
to a lesser classification. The latter depends on the quality of
the sampling and of the respondents' answers. But the major
limitation is that it is unclear what movements in the crime
figures really mean. Both data sets are indicators—but, at this
point in history, it is unclear what precisely they are indicating. The Uniform Crime Report data give information only on
reported crime, for example, and this shows "total crime"
trends only if the heroic assumption is made that the ratio of
reported to unreported crime is known (e.g., constant).
Beyond this, the totals are the result—simply—of adding
apples and pears. One robbery plus one homicide equals two
crimes; two incidents of shoplifting plus no robberies and no
homicides equals two crimes. Table 1 shows the crime rate in
a hypothetical small city for two separate years, and asks
whether the real crime rate has gone up or down.

The two data sets constitute only partial indicators—a
very narrow view of the "crime picture." Reliance in the Uniform Crime Report is placed on eight Part 1 or major crimes—
homicide, forcible rape, aggravated assault, robbery, burglary,

TABLE 1
Crime in a Hypothetical City: Up or Down?

Crime category	1974	1984
Homicide	2	1
Forcible rape	5	24
Aggravated assault	5	5
Robbery	7	6
Burglary	14	13
Larceny	15	1
Auto theft	13	10
Total	61	60

larceny, auto theft, and (now) arson. The National Crime Survey focuses on incidents of rape, robbery, assault, household burglary, and motor vehicle theft. Focusing on a narrow range of traditional crime categories, the Part 1 and the National Crime Survey data exclude important numbers from the critical crime totals—drug offenses, economic crime, terrorism and hijacking, for instance. Relying on incidents, the data ill define crime problems. Fixating on crime incidents, the data do not speak to the level of fear (or security) in communities. Such limitations in crime data measurement have not prevented the recurring crops of journalistic headlines reporting the latest quivers in the U.C.R. data; it is the exceptional journalist who emphasizes the limitations of the data. This brings us to a commonplace, but crucial, point about the public estimate of the size and trend of the crime problem. That estimate is based not only on data but also on impressions—impressions from television, from newspapers, from conversation, from experiences, and from a disjointed variety of ad hoc sources. The crime problem is only partly captured by the data from the measurement systems.

What is the extent of the crime problem in the United States? At least three considerations come to mind. First, there is an important but limited sense in which there is no single crime problem. Rather, there is a drug problem, a burglary problem, an organized crime problem, an economic crime problem . . . We can go farther. There is an important but limited sense in which there is no single drug problem. Rather, there is a cocaine problem, a heroin problem, a marijuana problem . . . We can go farther. There is an important but limited sense in which there is no single cocaine problem. Rather, there is . . . And so on. Second, the evidence of the two major data sets—U.C.R. and National Crime Survey—can be contradictory on crime trends. The former shows a dramatic general rise in the crime level from 1973 and through the seventies. The latter shows no such increase—but rather a general level trend. (In the year of writing [1983], the trend of both data sets is downward.) Third, the homicide rates indicate that the problem of violent crime is much larger in the United States than in other advanced countries. It is customary at this point in criminal justice writings to quote the truly staggering statistics showing that there are more homicides in any middle-sized U.S. city than in the whole of England with its population of some fifty million. It can be added that the evidence is that this disproportion has been a continuing feature of U.S. history. Cleveland had more murders than London in 1920, and Silberman reports that in 1828 Abraham Lincoln can be found warning of "the increasing disregard for law that prevades the country" (Silberman, 1978).

Resources Allocation

A tragedy of policing, despite the gains realized in recent years, is the proclivity to circle the wagons against change. American policing has made substantial gains since 1968 in such terms as improved average educational level of police officers, greater and more appropriate opportunities for minorities and women, greater attention paid to management thinking, increased use of automated data processing, and (as evidenced by the distance travelled away from the third-degree) humanizing general street procedures. Despite all this and despite the important exceptions represented by organizations like the Police Executive Research Forum and the National Organization of Black Law Enforcement Officers, the bulk of the police "community" remains skeptical, defensive, and unfriendly to suggestions for change. From behind the circled wagons come shots like "We are already doing that,"—"You don't understand,"—"Where has that ever been tried?"—"You are against police"—"We were doing that forty years ago." So it can only be with a heavy heart that one involved in the criminal justice system would offer suggestions for major change. It is more comfortable to stay within the circle; but that is not to serve the circle.

The hard facts are these. First, police agencies can make better use of their operational resources. Second, and more ir.portantly, the very process of police resources allocation decision-making is seriously flawed.

The present writer has written a number of articles and papers since 1975 substantiating, and expanding on, the contention that police agencies can make better use of their operational resources. The articles describe research results produced since the early seventies that document the need, and the opportunity, for revolutionizing the entire range of police operational practices like patrol and criminal investigations.

For those unfamiliar with these earlier writings, Chapter 2 summarizes and highlights the main threads of the argument concerning the misuse of police operational resources. Let us give only three examples here—response time, preventive patrol, and criminal investigations.

Police forces typically are organized and deployed on the false premise that police response time must be as rapid as possible in all cases. The Kansas City Response Time Study, described in Chapter 2, shows that response time includes not only police, but also citizen mobilization, time. Most rapid responses are unproductive, as, for example, when departments are geared up to respond in three minutes to the commercial robbery that has occurred an hour before. So the authors of that study conclude, first, that police response time will have negligible impact on crime outcome and, second, that more productive outcomes can be achieved if procedures can be developed to discriminate between emergency and nonemergency calls and if these are coordinated with patrol resource allocation. The Kansas City Preventive Patrol Study requires either a reconsideration of traditional preventive patrol or an explanation. For Police Chief Joseph McNamara, the study—while it did not show that "a visible police presence can have no impact on crime in selected circumstances"—meant that "routine patrol in marked police cars has little value in preventing crime or making citizens feel

safe" (McNamara, 1974). There may be a saturation point
where police manpower presence deters crime, and there may
be a low point where the absence of police spawns criminal
activity; but, at the middle range where police departments
now operate, manpower variations are irrelevant in terms of
preventing crime.

Other interpretations of the study are more conservative.
And what happens after the police get there? The Rand Study
of the Criminal Investigation Process reports that the most
important determinant of whether a case is solved is the information gathered by the immediately responding patrol officer. Of the remaining cases that are solved, the solutions usually result from routine police procedures. The message of
such studies is clear: traditional police operational approaches
misuse valuable resources.

Significant changes have been introduced in some police
agencies in the utilization of field resources. Managing Criminal Investigations (MCI) was a program introduced by many
agencies, for example, to give a more systematic character to
investigative operations. Another example, Managing Patrol
Operations (MPO), had similar aims for patrol. Departments
are to be congratulated for embracing such innovations. But
only the surface has been scratched.

The problem of allocating police resources appropriately
will not be solved until the public, policy-makers, and administrators have a sounder understanding of the nature of the
decision-making process. That existing techniques are deficient does constitute a difficulty. But the larger problem is that
our conceptualization of the process is incomplete. The character of its conceptualization inevitably conditions the manner in which an administrative or operating process is
regarded and treated. When the conceptualization is distorted,
the manner of managing the process is likely to be similarly
out of focus—no less with police resources allocation than
with any other process.

Three broad stages may be identified in the history of
police resources allocation decision-making. The first may be

termed the "ad hoc;" the second may be described as the "technical." A point of impasse has now been reached, where further progress cannot reasonably be anticipated without entering a third "conditional" stage. The techniques of the technical stage—it is suggested below—have proved flawed, just as did the methods of the ad hoc stage. Following comments suggest the reconceptualization required as a basis for the conditional stage.

The ad hoc stage of police resources allocation decision-making was characterized by an absence of formalized, quantitative procedures for determining needs, and a reliance on an intuitive and experiential approach. Kakalik refers to the technique as "Command Discretion" (Kakalik *et al.*, 1971 *(Aids to Decision-Making in Police Patrol)*). It was the approach used in the New York City Police Department prior to 1955 (and in many other jurisdictions, to be sure) and described in an October 16, 1967 memorandum to the Police Commissioner of that Department from the Commanding Officer of the Planning Bureau. "Prior to 1955, there was no established procedure within the New York City Police Department for the equitable distribution of the force to individual commands and precincts nor their assignment to specific posts. Members were apportioned to the various branches of the department according to actual and predetermined needs based on commanding officers' experience and knowledge. Individual patrol precinct commanders, for the most part, determined the posts to be covered and the men to be assigned thereto based on their personal knowledge of the command."

The technical stage of police resources allocation decision-making has been characterized by the use of quantitative techniques for discharging what has been viewed as management's difficult but narrow (and technical) dilemma of determining how manpower and other resources are to be assigned among competing geographical areas and among alternative functions. Two main sets of techniques have been utilized. Firstly, proportional distribution techniques have been employed in equalizing among geographical subdivisions either police workload (through the use of workload formulae) or the provisions of police protective services (through hazard formulae). A well-thumbed account of such beat studies may be found in standard textbooks such as O. W. Wilson's and Roy McLaren's *Police Administration*. Secondly, mathematical (or computer) modelling approaches—encouraged by recommendations of the 1967 President's Commission on Law Enforcement and Administration of Justice—have been applied to manpower allocation problems. Four main types of such computer models can be distinguished in analytic models for patrol car allocation, simulation models for analyzing patrol policy issues, analytic models for designing patrol beat boundaries, and linear programming optimization models for minimizing patrol tours required within the constraint of a user-specified car requirement per hour.

The characteristic that distinguishes the technical from the conditional stage is that police resources allocation decision-making was seen in the former as being essentially an apolitical process. The decision-making was viewed as directed entirely toward technical, program purposes such as equalizing hazards or reducing response time. It was not understood as serving any direct political ends, e.g., satisfying a particular interest-group demand; working toward "saving" small businesses in a deteriorating neighborhood; and so on. Essentially, then, the technical stage sees the decision-making as politics-free or value-free.

Both the proportional distribution and the mathematical modelling approaches, however, have proven to be of limited utility to practitioners, contrary to the hopes of the technical enthusiasts. Reasons lie partly in the particular features of the approaches developed; they also lie in the assumptions implied about the allocation process—the way in which the process has been conceptualized. Others may suggest additional reasons, such as the extent of receptivity to change in police agencies. Concerning the first reason, for example, the workload/hazard formulae equalize workload (or hazards) without reference to other important performance measures; and they can actually distort allocations. Larson points to the correlation between sufficiently policed areas and the greater number of reported crimes and arrests which could be interpreted as indicating a need for more personnel in an area already relatively overallocated (Larson, 1972). The computer models, too, have proven misdirected, relying too heavily (although not exclusively) on response time as a crucial performance objective—conventional wisdom that must be viewed as having been overturned. This wisdom held that police operations should be managed to ensure that calls for service are responded to as quickly as possible. Bieck has shown response time to be significant only in a minority of cases (Bieck *et al.*, 1977, 1979, 1980); his Kansas City Response Time Study has been replicated, with similar results in Jackson-Duvall, San Diego, and Peoria (Spelman *et al.*, 1981). The relevance of the other intermediate indicators is no clearer. Here, Chaiken's comment should be recalled—"To the extent that performance measures of importance to police administrators (e.g., deterrence of crime, apprehension of criminal offenders) are omitted from the [resource allocation] program, it is not because they are deemed unimportant but rather because there is no known way to estimate them" (Chaiken, 1975).

The second set of reasons center around the conceptualization of resources allocation implied by such techniques. In describing these techniques and the literature, Chapter 3 also documents how the criminal justice literature treats only a special aspect of the decision-making process. The literature makes the false assumption that the process is entirely technical or professional. Inappropriately, it assumes that the process is apolitical. This is unrealistic; police managers in the United States typically operate in a political context. Empirical evidence is presented in Chapter 4, showing that police resources allocation decision-making is conducted within a context of the tugs and pulls of political and interest-group pressures.

Needed is a wider conceptualization of the process—one that is here called the conditional. Basically, this view recog-

nizes the reality of both the "technical" and "political" considerations and the forces impacting on the process. These
forces, it argues, are not fortuitous accidents. Rather, their
strengths can be estimated; their influences can be manipulated for the public or other good; the forces can be analyzed
and controlled. The conditional conception recognizes the
importance of conditions—of the underlying factors helpful
in describing, explaining, and predicting how allocation decisions are made. Rather than relying merely on the reasons or
rationale expressed by the allocators themselves, it focuses
also on the more basic forces—paralleling (as it were) Adam
Smith's "invisible hand" explanation of the functioning of the
economy. One aim of this book is to lay a foundation for such
a conditional theory of police resources allocation.

Needed also is the recognition that the objectives of the
resources allocation process can be set by the administrator,
and these purposes need not be confined within traditional
limits. Consider each element of the activity—"resources" and
then "allocation." Viewing resources only in terms of manpower totals, a working assumption of current proportional
distribution and mathematical modelling approaches is that "a
police officer is a police officer is a police officer." On the contrary, some police officers have capabilities not possessed by
others, e.g., the capability of speaking a particular language,
of understanding a particular subculture, of being educated,
of being experienced in particular kinds of street work. Some
functions and areas may have greater need for some capabilities than for others. Allocation approaches that consider only
manpower totals leave this personnel-type consideration until
later. But it is possible to go farther, transforming Resources
Allocation approaches into systems for Capabilities Utilization.

Allocation or utilization can be understood as consisting
of three major types. For convenience, we will call these
Micro-Resources Allocation, Mini-Resources Allocation, and
Macro-Resources Allocation. The allocation techniques noted
above—the proportional distribution and the mathematical

modelling—have been of the first type. The assumption has been that they operate within the shorter term when neither the purpose nor the essential structure of the agency is changed. They move pieces on an unchanging chess board. This is fine as far as it goes; but more is needed. Mini-Resources Allocation recognizes that the board itself can be changed. Not only resources but also the very purposes and operating character of the agency can be changed in this "longer-term." Macro-Resources Allocation, going beyond the individual department, considers resources allocation among a number of departments in a region or country. It recognizes that not only the board but also the entire game can be changed. It is under the latter two headings that we can move to consideration of the new form of police agency.

The point about changing the conceptualization of the process is not merely that the technical concept encourages policy-makers and managers to work with allocation techniques that are inappropriate for the circumstances. It is not merely that the managers are being asked to use round pegs in square holes—that they are being asked to make political decisions apolitically. It is not merely that they are ignoring the underlying conditions that shape the decisions, missing a bet for the public good. The point is that acceptance of the conditional conceptualization encourages not only a realistic but also an open style of decision-making. Resources allocation becomes, as it should become, purpose-oriented. This will enable us to reach a new era which will require the new form of police agency.

New Form of Police Agency

Up close, each police department has its own individuality. Viewed from a distance, however, the commonalities among police agencies are more striking than individual differences. From afar we can see this country's more than 16,500 police agencies—some as big as armies or corporations but most consisting of only a handful of people—unevenly pro-

ceeding over the past hundred or so years from the ad hoc to
the professional model. Some have not yet started the journey;
others are well advanced.

In the last century, police work was seen as unskilled, a
job requiring no training, no education, and no special talents
beyond common sense and an able body. Police institutions—
here characterized as ad hoc—were firmly controlled by local
politicians and machines. Lawlessness, corruption, and inef-
ficiency were reportedly general, and the example of the large
cities comes to mind (e.g., see Fogelson, 1977). The professional model—spurred by recurring scandals and pioneered
by August Vollmer, Bruce Smith, and O. W. Wilson—was
directed toward operating effectiveness and efficiency based
on knowledge, service, and autonomy. In an earlier time, this
drive toward effectiveness/efficiency of operations took the
form of an increased emphasis on paramilitarism. In the past
several decades, there has been a movement toward such features as better management, improved training, more effective
use of equipment, more education, and greater integrity.
Above all, this drive has aimed toward professional autonomy, toward insulation from local and partisan politics. In this
country, the culmination was reached in the "Great Society"
establishment in 1968 of the Law Enforcement Assistance
Administration and of the efforts of the U.S. Government to
facilitate the operating effectiveness of the criminal justice
system.

Dissatisfaction is being felt with the professional model,
however. There has been talk and some action about community-based policing and accountability. It is well-established that police agencies are important substantive policy-
making agencies of government (e.g., Remington, 1980), and
the need for openness in police policy-making and administration has been urged. A well-known prescription for police
agencies, for example, is Kenneth Culp Davis' view that what
is needed is to confine, check, and structure discretion
through such means as open plans and open policy statements

(Davis, 1971). Meanwhile, private policing proliferates as it fills in those societal needs not met by the public police. There is a groping toward a new form. There is a seeking for a new stage that, without denying the achievements of agencies striving for the professional model, is appropriate for community and societal goals within the conditions of particular times and places. This we will call, arbitrarily and modestly, the "new form."

Some may wish to become more fanciful and explain this progression of police institutional forms in the United States—this progression to the ad hoc, to the professional, and to the new form. The more fanciful may imagine a societal need for order maintenance that parallels in principle Maslow's hierarchy of needs for individuals. Predominant societal conditions do differ considerably between these phases of policing, and a relevant sociological or technological revolution can be described as inaugurating each stage. When it was simple, society in the first stage had no need for formal police institutions. It could still rely on such mechanisms as had proven effective for the medieval English village, for instance. The relevant technological revolution that inaugurated the ad hoc stage of police institutions was the industrial revolution, with such developments as the growth of super-cities, of populations, and of mobility. In this second stage, the need for order maintenance required full-time agencies; but still it could be met by common sense or unspecialized police procedures and by untrained personnel. Societal needs for greater effectiveness in the second and at the beginning of the third stage could be realized by the use of paramilitary approaches—people disciplined but untrained in police procedures. The third stage was induced by such revolutionary changes as the rise of the professions, the development of relevant technology such as the automobile and the radio, by the accelerating changes of an ever more mobile society, and by the activities and fates in the United States of the urban political machines. This was the period of the professional model.

The futurists have described, some in glittering prose, the profound changes society is now undergoing. Let us take only two examples. Alvin Toffler described in 1980 the Third Wave: "A new civilization is emerging in our lives, and blind men everywhere are trying to suppress it . . . The dawn of this new civilization . . . is the central event—the key to understanding the years immediately ahead. It is an event as profound as that First Wave of change unleashed ten thousand years ago by the invention of agriculture, or the earthshaking Second Wave touched off by the Industrial Revolution. We are the children of the next transformation, the Third Wave" (Toffler, 1980). John Naisbitt described in 1982 what he called the mega-trends, ten new directions transforming our lives (Naisbitt, 1982). "We are living in the time of the parenthesis, the time between eras," he explains. So the fanciful will ask how we can suppose that our professional model for policing will be adequate for the new age. He will challenge us to read these futurists, to think about policing, and he will tell us that our own flight of fancy has been to ignore the reality of changing societal needs.

But it is not necessary to be fanciful to recognize that new perspectives are needed. Let us return to terra firma. The more thoughtful are already questioning the sufficiency of contemporary reform efforts and of the professional model to meet contemporary and emerging societal needs. Let Herman Goldstein speak for the need for a new approach. "The answer, I believe, is that we have been preoccupied with building a superstructure without having laid an adequate foundation; that the whole reform movement in policing has been short-sighted in focusing almost exclusively on improving the police establishment (its organization, staffing, equipment, and so on) without having given adequate attention to some serious underlying problems that grow out of the basic arrangements for policing in our society. Paramount among these are the ambiguity surrounding the police function and the numerous conflicts and contradictions inherent in police operations" (Goldstein, 1977). The clearest symptom and the gravest consequence of this insufficiency is the persistence of the crime problem.

The professional, it may be pointed out, is a model with varieties of meaning. Here it is understood to suggest a form with two major characteristics. One is a drive for effectiveness-efficiency founded on autonomy; another is the same drive based on professional knowledge and the service ideal. Professional autonomy is said to rest on a monopoly of skill. Professional knowledge rests on mastery of an esoteric, abstract, and codified body of principles, according to Walder, and he described the professional subculture as the means for maintaining the service ideal (Walder, 1976). Some argue that the police fail to meet the criteria of a profession (e.g., Feville and Juris, 1976; Decotiis and Kochan, 1978). But that argument is not really the point. The major problem is what the model implies, and what it does not emphasize, about the police institution. The model implies a shutting out of the non-professional, such as the elected official, from police policy-making and implementation—from partnership in the setting of goals and in execution. The model does not emphasize institutional purpose; on the contrary, professionalism has a tendency to accent process. That argument also misses the point in that much in the professional model is in the public interest and is an essential ingredient of the new form. Major among these is the capacity for utilizing research results and new perspectives, a feature described here as organizational creativity.

What would be the general shape of the new form? Before we begin, a reservation must be entered. A ragged and general progression of police institutional forms has been suggested—the ad hoc, the professional, the new form. The term "ragged" is used to reflect the fact that the phases are not clear-cut stages: for example, they share important features. It may make more sense for some communities mired in the ad hoc to strive, not for the new form, but for the more attainable professional model. For those communities insisting on retaining the anomaly in this atomic–computer age of a one-

person police institution, there may be no realistic alternative
than to stay in the ad hoc stage. For those wishing the com-
forts of a "Surrey with the fringe on top," there is no opportunity to travel at 55 miles per hour. All this is to say no more
than that improvement plans and generalities must be tailored to local realities and differences.

The new form of police agency would be structured,
staffed, and managed so that it has two major capabilities
beyond those of the professional model. Possession of these
capabilities, in conjunction with a third which is part of the
professional model, would ensure evolution of the police
institution into the required new form.

The first is the capacity for developing—in partnership
with other public and private agencies—workable purposes,
plans, and policies for realizing higher levels of order, law,
and justice in the community. This we can call Policy Formulation. The second is the capacity for mobilizing and leading
agencies and individuals in order to achieve order enhancement, with an emphasis on working not only directly but also
indirectly through other societal organizations. This we will
call Policy Leadership. The third is the capacity for utilizing
research results and new perspectives as much as possible in
its thinking about its "doing" activities—the capacity for
being creative. This we will consider under the heading of
Policy Administration. Let us look at each in turn, providing
examples of the differences.

Concerning policy formulation, the new form of police
agency would be capable of providing leadership to other
public and private agencies in the community in the cooper-
ative development of realistic long- and short-term plans for
sub-elements of the community and for the community as a
whole. These plans would be realistic in addressing order
maintenance problems proactively, rather than on the reactive
basis now so common. They would provide not only for programmatic activity and community initiative, but also for
whatever institutional adjustments (for example, in the working of the criminal justice system) are helpful in realizing

objectives. This would entail the new police agency having more than merely the skill to help the community develop the total cost-benefit (social as well as economic) implications of alternatives in maintaining various order levels at particular locations, and identifying optimal mixes of resources utilization. It would entail the political skill needed to persuade, cajole, and induce others to shape plans in the public interest. Police agencies cannot become merely research organizations; rather, armed with the results of competent research melded with their experience and the sense of the practical, the new agency must be as cunning as a fox and as deadly as a snake in developing workable and meaningful crime control plans in partnership with elected officials and community organizations. This would also (and importantly) imply accountability of the police agency, including the institution's capacity to evaluate and to report on order level changes in communities and situations.

Among the differences in this respect between the new form and the contemporary police institution, two should be underscored. First, beyond such general and operationally unhelpful prescriptions as "to protect and serve" (a statement of purpose shared at least by the navy, the army, and the local sanitation department), the actions of contemporary police institutions are little shaped by precise specifications of purpose. Later the results of two surveys of police practices are referenced, one being a survey of United States police agencies serving populations over 100,000 and the other of agencies in a selected state with populations over 5,000. The agencies were asked (among other things) for statements of purpose for their patrol, investigation, and traffic activities. The majority of the respondents reported that they have "no purpose." Second, "order maintenance" is a satisfactory characterization of the purpose of policing insofar as the present administrator is not held responsible for more than maintaining the status quo of order. The new form of police agency would be required to go farther, being responsible for the purposive activity of order enhancement. The burden would be added of making a gain, a "profit," for society.

Let us take two examples of policy formulation, the new level of practical police thinking, that will be required. This will illustrate the difference in service between the new, and the existing, form of police agency.

The first example focuses on an incident of police resources allocation decision-making. Imagine, if you will, a street of delightful specialty stores—one little store specializing in various kinds of coffees, another in pastries, another in books, another in crafts, and so on. Imagine that one night one of the store owners, working late, is robbed and murdered. The outcry from the other store owners is loud, claiming that unless they are better protected their customers will be driven away and they will be forced out of business. "Give us more police," they demand. How will the old police agency respond? We will see later that, in theory, police workload is allocated in proportion to a standard such as relative demand for service or the minimization of average police response time. In practice, such theory is likely to be bent by the practical politics of responding to the outcry and of the "importance" of the street in question to the city.

The new police agency will have a clear sense of purpose, and thus a sounder basis for making a decision about allocating additional resources to that street. Beyond general prescriptions, the new police agency will have a street-by-street understanding of its own purposes, developed in consultation with elected officials. In the street of specialty stores, for instance, its major goal might be to induce a feeling of safety among out-of-town residents because that commercial development is important to the regional reputation of the city. Such an understanding of purpose would shape the resource allocation response. A paradox of contemporary policing is that, while they are the most action-oriented of organizations, police agencies typically are adrift in an ocean of undefined purpose; and they go where the strongest winds blow.

The new police form could also be expected to reach its decision on a sounder information base. In the example quoted, for instance, it could not be expected to remain innocent of such realities as the profit margins typical for the sort of businesses at issue, the capability of the businesses for self-help, the impact on order maintenance of diverting resources from elsewhere, and the likelihood of increased resources having an influence on the situation. Intuitive decision-making is not at all to be despised. But, if based on fact and logic, decisions in the new form of police agency will need less shielding under a cloak such as "official business" or "at this time I am not at liberty to disclose." Such agencies can become—not completely but more—open.

The second example relates to crime prevention. Imagine that a group wishes to build a new shopping mall in a fringe area. Reacting to a request, some police agencies can provide developers with a very useful—but limited—range of advice on security implications. The extent to which they are capable of advising on the defensible space implications of architectural plans and on innovative methods of security planning is problematic. The extent to which they can anticipate the order maintenance impact of such projects, seeking to influence actions before the building is cast in concrete, is even more problematic.

The new police agency will not only provide these services well. Along the lines laid down in its joint planning with elected officials, it will be actively concerned with order enhancement in locations evaluated as significant for the development of the city. Among the alternatives it may consider one might be to encourage the city's economic development agency or Chamber of Commerce to seek arrangements to facilitate a particular kind of business (e.g., a factory) or public activity (e.g., a park) at a particular location—for a specified order enhancement objective and in accordance with an orderly plan of community priorities; examples of other candidate alternatives will readily occur to the reader. The point is that the new form of police agency will be truly proactive in its crime prevention: it will seek ways to turn back the tide of community disorder, following plans developed openly and jointly with elected officials.

Concerning policy leadership, the new form of police agency will be—it was noted—one capable of mobilizing and inducing community action toward realizing higher levels of order, law, and justice in its community. The primary capability will be that of achieving community order enhancement goals through others. These others will include the other elements of the criminal justice system (courts, probation, corrections, and so on), private security, social service and other agencies impacting on criminals and criminality, other public entities of the various levels of government, private businesses, politicians, journalists, and private individuals. Implied in this is that the new form of police agency must develop a leadership role in both its criminal justice system and its community. To do this, it must earn the "respect" it needs.

Let us take two examples of policy leadership—of how the new form of police agency would work toward its objectives primarily through other agencies and individuals. The first example of working through others is that of private security. In the United States, there are far more private, than public, police officers. They guard persons, facilities, and activities covering the gamut from the trivial (like golf courses) to the critical (like atomic plants); they range from the un- to the ultra-sophisticated. Three major studies have analyzed private security in the United States and explored the relationship of private with public police—the 1971 Rand Study, the 1976 study of the National Advisory Committee on Criminal Justice Standards and Goals, and the 1984 Hallcrest Systems study. Two major themes stand out. The operating relationships between the two forms of "policing" are, to be diplomatic, tenuous where they are existent. Private security constitutes, in the words of the National Advisory Committee, a "massive resource . . . for crime prevention and reduction," (National Advisory Commission, 1976) and this resource is not effectively utilized by police agencies. The new form of police agency would actively seek to use all such resources. Certainly, an "inward-looking" professionalism would not be permitted to discourage coordination.

The second is the example of the private individual. The literature of police-community relations is immense, and there has surely been mighty progress in this respect since the mid-sixties. But gross problems remain. Complaints about discriminatory policing are voiced in some communities by minority groups such as blacks and gays and by females; the history of the Guardian Angels, whatever the merits of the particular case, is also very instructive; and so on. Turning away from what some may consider to be special groups, why do so many citizens delay in reporting incidents to the police? The Kansas City Response Time Study described the following "pattern" delays—displaying apathy, feeling uncertain about police assistance, contacting security, investigating the crime scene, telephoning another person, and waiting or observing the situation. Clearly, not all the blame (and perhaps not even most of it) can be laid at the feet of the police. But do some police agencies not give out a double message? "Call us if you see anything suspicious" is one message; another is "So what do you want us to do?" or "Well, what have you done about it?" The new form of police agency should have the analytical and other capacity that is required to lick this difficult problem, mobilizing more individuals and groups in their own best interests.

Concerning policy administration, the critical characteristic is the creative capacity of utilizing research and new perspectives to the optimal extent in shaping the agency's own actions. The day will come—perhaps in twenty years—when criminal justice practice will be research-based in the same way that medicine now is. The physician still practices his/her art; but, unlike the nineteenth century doctors, there are presently few medical practitioners who will claim that their practice is not research-based. Even those physicians who do not keep current with research results would surely be expected to acknowledge that it would be better if they did. When theory and practice have developed sufficiently, criminal justice practice will become similarly research-based. The practitioner, instead of being confined to his own rich experience base, will have more solid information. The police institution must adapt for this coming reality. Some police agencies will become the "teaching hospitals" of the police profession; but even the meanest police agency must be capable of utilizing research results fully.

This feature, creativity, is consistent with the professional model; acting synergistically with policy formulation and policy leadership, its contribution is essential for the flowering of the new form of police agency. A prime characteristic of activities in the new form of agency—surely—must be creativity. Bureaucratic rigidity and adherence to procedure are dangers for all sizeable institutions, particularly public agencies. In a society such as we face in coming years, such rigidity in a critical agency like policing can be expected to be especially harmful to realization of societal goals. The solution must be active. Needed will be an emphasis on creativity as pronounced as the tendency hitherto has been to adherence to established procedures.

Examples of the relevance of research have already been noted and more are given in Chapter 2 on studies relating to police operations; an example of a new perspective is offered in Chapter 4. No significant area of policing should have been unaffected by some research results achieved during the past decade—anti-corruption management, narcotics control, police program performance measurement, and so on. So let us be content to give two brief examples concerning the need for creativity. The first is the deterrence of theft of clothes from department stores and the second is the reduction of thefts of shopping carts from supermarkets. Private security is to be congratulated on the "cleverness" of its approaches in both cases. In the former, attached to the clothes are devices that can "only" be removed by a special machine. In the latter, posts set close together in the parking lots deter customers from taking shopping carts to their cars. How would such problems have been resolved if they could have been left to public police agencies? A less creative approach, for instance, might have been preventive patrol in the areas concerned. In the coming era, such problems are liable to appear relatively simple.

Do public police agencies not already have such capabilities? Of course, some police officers and some police agencies are extremely sophisticated; but the new form of police agency, with these three features acting together, is yet to be realized. That some traces of this new form may be found in a few progressive police departments, while encouraging, is hardly convincing. Do tigers have the capability of analyzing, synthesizing, and reflecting? No, but they do have a thinking function that bears strong resemblances. We can be happy that some of our police agencies are tigers; but we have in mind a higher form.

THE AGENDA

This book, then, constitutes an analysis and a policy agenda that centers on a subject critical for crime control—the use and misuse of police resources. First, it is concerned with resources allocation decision-making. It describes current techniques and practices for allocating such resources. It provides fresh information on allocation practices, and it provides a new framework for understanding and developing allocation techniques. Second, it describes significant aspects of the new form of police agency that are required if police resources are to be utilized effectively and if society is to address the crime problem. It outlines the character of the new form and indicates policy steps for implementation.

The views presented here are based on an interdisciplinary approach, melding the results of survey, of economic, and of criminal justice research. Survey research data have been collected from a survey of United States cities with popula-

tions over 100,000, from a survey of communities in the State
of Virginia with populations over 5,000, and from participant
observation case studies. Economic inputs have been developed by applying some of the basic conceptual tools of
microeconomics. Reliance has also been placed on the extensive and growing criminal justice research and other literature. Finally and inevitably, the views have been conditioned
by the writer's own experiences—as Special Assistant to the
Police Commissioner in the New York City Police Department, as Director of the Police Division in the National Institute of Justice at the U.S. Department of Justice, as Chairman
and Associate Professor of the Department of Administration
of Justice and Public Safety at Virginia Commonwealth University, and as a consultant for police agencies across the
country.

The specifics of the survey on police resources allocation
decision-making should be noted (Farmer, 1981). The survey
data presented here were collected from a mail survey, from
follow-up telephone interviews, and from participant observation studies in three sites. The mail survey was conducted,
as has been noted, in U.S. cities with populations over 100,000
and in Virginia communities with populations over 5,000. The
former is referenced as the National Sample; the latter is
described as the Virginia Sample. The 39-item questionnaire
was developed with the advice of a committee of police managers, pretested in two sites, and administered (with a follow-
up for nonrespondents) in June–August 1981. The response
rate was 78% for the national survey and 82% for the Virginia
sample. A telephone sampling of nonrespondents was taken
to test the representativeness of the response. This was supplemented by follow-up telephone interviews with 36% of the
respondents, selected on the basis of their questionnaire
response. A structured instrument was utilized for that purpose. Participant observation case studies were conducted in
Summer 1981. These were supplemented by less structured
visits to other sites. At each of the major sites, case history

information was sought on the characteristics of actual resource allocation decisions made during the past year in the respective cities. Interviews were conducted with the chief, with other department personnel, and with city officials. Other departmental personnel included the head of the planning and research unit, and representative line commanders such as the Chief of Patrol, and selected area commanders and supervisors; selected city officials included elected and appointed persons. To facilitate freedom of response, assurances were given that individual departmental and city results would be kept confidential and that only aggregated results would be reported.

The book is divided into four major sections—Policy Administration, Policy Formulation, Policy Leadership, and Policy Beginnings. The choice of the first three headings has been made to reflect the major characteristics of the new form of agency, and the order of their presentation has been chosen to represent what for many would be a natural evolution for an agency passing to the culmination of the professional model and beyond to the new form. The term "policy" is used throughout to emphasize the necessity of concentrating on the fundamental or macro arrangements for allocating resources and for establishing the new form. It underscores the need to look at the "woods" (the basic arrangements of the new form) before tackling the "trees" (the administrative details, the inevitable nitty-gritty difficulties), and in so doing it runs counter to the natural but impossible "criminal justice impulse" for instant results. It is this set of basic policies or approaches that constitutes a genuine agenda for communities wanting effective crime control.

At one level, this book is a twin institutional "biography." It analyzes police resources allocation decision-making; and it also provides an analysis of the total police institution by means of its account of the new form. Concerning resources allocation decision-making, it indicates some problematic results of contemporary allocation practices; it outlines the development and nature of present allocation approaches and techniques; and it analyzes the political context of such allocation decision-making, presenting a reconceptualization of the resources allocation process that addresses the factors underlying the extent to which allocation decisions are politicized. It then describes the sort of realistic planning that must be a part of the resources allocation process, beginning at the neighborhood level; it outlines a new view of police resources allocation decision-making, using the viewpoint of economics literature; and it describes a "planning-budgeting-resources allocation" approach that forms a sound basis for upgrading resources allocation decision-making and results.

Concerning the total police institution, the book depicts lacks in the present police institution; and it gives an additional view of the problem—the unfortunate emphasis on process, for example. It outlines the pervasive role of politics in contemporary police decision-making, and presents the beginning of an approach for coping more effectively. It goes further, suggesting how police agencies can overcome their malaise by appropriate emphasis on realistic and purpose-oriented planning; it notes how politicians are failing in their management of the police function, and suggests practical measures for better results; and it describes present deficiencies in police management by indicating how police managers can come to grips with the more fundamental needs of their institutions through pursuing the features of the new form of police agency. But in the end, these two "biographies"—these analyses of two institutional elements—come together, because effective resources allocation decision-making and the effective police institution are really opposite sides of the same coin.

At another level, this publication is a call to arms. It is a call to action based on the three contentions noted at the beginning of this chapter. First, crime can, and needs to be, more effectively controlled. Second, police resources can be more effectively used, and they must be better utilized if the crime control problem is to be addressed. Third, only by pursuing a policy agenda that works toward a new form of policy agency can this more effective utilization be realized. It is a call to arms because we have the knowledge and the skill to do better; we must do better.

PART I

Policy Administration

*"Ah, take one consideration with
another—A policeman's lot is not a
happy one."*
GILBERT (AND SULLIVAN)

"Justice without wisdom is impossible."
FROUDE

CHAPTER 2

The Science of Policing

A cumulative message of modern police research is clear and compelling. The traditional police institution and the traditional structure for using resources on the street are failing, and policy and administrative arrangements for managing field services require comprehensive restructuring. Police research has raised discomforting questions about traditional practices. It has indicated opportunities for upgrading the professional model. Beyond this, the research suggests the need for the new form of police agency that can marshal extra-departmental resources jointly to plan and to achieve order enhancement.

This research message that the police institution and the management of field resources require fundamental reconstruction has been repeatedly offered by the present writer and is becoming ever more widely accepted in police agencies and elsewhere. "The contemporary police institution—the complex of programs, systems, and job repertoires maintained by police management for 'determining' what officers do—remains less than adequate in meeting society's needs" (Farmer, 1980). Thus began a paper delivered at Cambridge

University in 1979, specifying how police agencies could build on the police research questions and pointers to reshape the nature and upgrade the caliber of police field services. "Police agencies are at the beginning of a revolution in operating practices. The question is not whether the revolution will occur but how long a period is required for percolation" (Farmer, 1978).

This message is summarized by describing research undertaken since the early seventies on police field operations. Reliance has been placed in this description on a paper published by the writer on "Thinking About Research: The Contribution of Social Science Research to Contemporary Policing" in the journal *Police Studies* (Farmer, 1981). Four headings are utilized—response strategy, preventive patrol, criminal investigation, and scientific and analytic capability.

This account is possible because of a radical contribution made by the sixties and seventies to policing and to crime control—the laying of the foundations of a science of policing. Compared with the massive need for the practical results of police research, the beginning has been slight. But compared with the primitive level of the knowledge of police matters less than two decades ago, the beginning has been significant.

RESPONSE STRATEGY

On the street and in the communications center, the dominant theme of the organization and management of police operations is to respond as rapidly as possible to incoming calls for service. Scarcity of resources compels some delay in some cases, when incidents have to wait for a police car to become available or when an obvious priority (such as a bank robbery in progress) takes precedence over a less urgent incident. The basic principle, nevertheless, is to get there as soon as possible. The main activity of police is patrol—involving cars roving on patrol, not only for order maintenance and crime prevention purposes, but also to be in good position to respond rapidly: they are "out there," ready to spring. Another main function of patrol activity is to respond to calls for service—citizens requesting help or service, usually by telephone. Communications centers, increasingly equipped with computer aids, are designed to move the request as rapidly as possible to the appropriate car. "Although many departments try to assign calls in order of urgency, the majority of schemes they use make only the general distinction between calls that obviously require immediate, mobile response by police officers and those for which mobile sworn officer response can be delayed ... Operators collect only enough information from the caller to classify the incoming call to the dispatcher ... " The amount of information passed on "does not provide enough information for officers to make a proper decision about the most appropriate response nor to prepare themselves to respond properly when they arrive at the scene" (Farmer, Michael T., 1981). "We will have a car there right away." "We will have somebody there as soon as possible." Ironically, the practice of aiming for an immediate response ensures that every response is late; a call answered in thirty seconds, for instance, is "thirty seconds" later than "right away."

This basic operating principle of police operations—that police response must be designed to be as rapid as possible in virtually all cases in order to achieve satisfactory crime control results—was challenged by the Kansas City Response Time and related studies. The research suggests the need to revamp operational practices, on both effectiveness and cost grounds, along the lines of a differential response strategy. This is explained below.

The landmark study, changing our understanding of the nature of the significance of police response time, was the Response Time Study conducted in the Kansas City Police Department (Bieck *et al.*, 1977, 1979, 1980). The study's purpose was to analyze the relationship of response time to the outcomes of on-scene criminal apprehension, witness availability, citizen satisfaction, and the frequency of citizen injuries in connection with crime and noncrime incidents, and to identify problems and patterns in reporting crime and requesting police assistance. Through the use of civilian observers, analysis of communications center tapes, and interviews with victims and witnesses, approximately 7,000 citizen-generated calls for service processed through the system were analyzed. Unlike earlier studies, this research did not rely on officer self-reporting.

The study indicated the need to reconceptualize response time. Rather than thinking of response time merely as the interval between the moment the police agency receives a call for service and the arrival time of the squad car, it is necessary to include the citizen mobilization interval—the time it takes the citizen to report the incident. The citizen mobilization interval, the forgotten element in response time, is large in Kansas City—48.1 percent of the total response time for Part I, 51.7 percent for Part II, and 49.3 percent for noncrime, incidents. This reporting interval is more significant in some types of incidents than others; in commercial robberies, for instance, it is particularly long.

The study also showed the need to reassess the significance of response time. Much effort after the 1967 President's Commission on Law Enforcement and Administration of Justice was centered on reducing response time (the operations research activity, for instance); millions of dollars were invested in computer-aided dispatch systems, and many departments still utilize average response times as performance criteria. The reality is that rapid response is important in only a minority of incidents.

First, most crime calls do not reflect emergency situations. The Kansas City study reported that 62% of the Part I crimes and 51% of all crimes are not discovered until after the perpetrators have left the scene, and rapid response to effect arrests or locate witnesses is largely irrelevant. Second, even among cases where witnesses or victims are involved while the crime is occurring (rather than incidents, like many burglaries, discovered after the event), the impact of police response is often nullified by delays in citizen reporting. In some 50% of the involvement cases in the Kansas City study, citizens delayed more than five minutes before calling the police—making rapid police response irrelevant to arrest or witness availability. (An involvement crime is defined as one in which a citizen saw, heard, or became involved between the time the suspect began committing the crime and the citizen became free from involvement in the crime.) Involvement crimes were reported quickly enough for rapid response to be potentially effective in only 18% of total crime calls. Third, the percentage of arrests attributable to rapid response is small—in this study in only 3.7% of the Part I and 5.6% of the Part II crimes. Many on-scene arrests could have been made regardless of police response, because of (as the report points out) information provided by the victim or other person on the scene, apprehension of the suspect by a private citizen or security guard, immobility due to suspect injury, or because the suspect voluntarily submitted to arrest.

Two implications in the report on this study deserve emphasis here. First, the authors concluded that "because of the time citizens take to report crimes, police response time will have negligible impact on crime outcomes." Second, they indicate that "if procedures can be developed to discriminate accurately between emergency and nonemergency calls, more productive response-related outcomes can be achieved if coordinated with patrol resource allocation" (Bieck et al., 1980).

The findings of this study may no longer be questioned as representing the experience of only Kansas City. Establishing the generalizability of the data, the key component of the response time continuum—the citizen mobilization interval—has been measured in other jurisdictions. This has been done by the Police Executive Research Forum in Jacksonville-Duvall, San Diego, and Peoria (Spelman et al., 1981). The data support the Kansas City findings. The replication study also explored further the reasons for these citizen delays. The Kansas City study identified two categories of reasons for citizen delays—problems and patterns. "Problems" were defined as

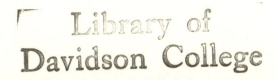

controllable hindrances encountered by an individual, and the most frequently cited problem was trouble with public communication—primarily the unavailability of a telephone. "Patterns" were defined as voluntary actions or attitudes affecting the decision to call the police. The most frequently cited pattern was talking to another person, usually to obtain advice or to seek assistance or additional information. Problems and patterns were found to be more strongly affected by situational factors (the type of incident) than by the type of individual reporting the incident. The importance of exploring this further lies in shedding light on opportunities for reducing the citizens' mobilization interval by some means such as an intensive public education program.

The impression should not be given, however, that the Kansas City Response Time Study and its replications currently stand alone on the topic of response time. In fact, for a review of the literature, see Volume I of the Response Time Analysis reports. The City of Wilmington, during its Split Force experiment (Tien *et al.*, 1979), concluded—as an example—that citizen satisfaction is a function of expectation and what the citizen is willing to accept. For example, a 30-minute delay in response to a noncritical call is normally acceptable if the citizen is formally advised of the delay. They also found that in Wilmington some 86% of all calls for service are noncritical. The Police Foundation also reported (Pate, 1976) on three surveys finding no relation between response time and arrest rates, contrary to Herbert Isaac's research for the 1967 President's Commission. It indicated that citizen satisfaction depended not on rapid response, but on the difference between observed and expected response.

Faced with these research results, some agencies have begun—and all should begin—to introduce a differential police response strategy. Whether or not the same title is used, such a strategy is based on the notion that police response should be tailored both in character and timing to the nature of the situation. Tying up resources to get there as quickly as possible is unnecessary and wasteful, preventing an agency from making alternative and better utilization of its scarce capability. A differential police response strategy contemplates a variety of responses based on the nature of the request for service—immediate, planned delay (an officer will be there in thirty minutes), appointment, walk-in, mail-in, telephone reporting, referring the caller to another agency, and no response, for example. Further, the response may be made by various categories of personnel, such as sworn and civilian. It is granted that many police agencies for some time have made extensive use of some alternative responses—telephone reporting, for instance. But the use of a complete differential response strategy is a different matter.

The Police Executive Research Forum and the City of Birmingham Police Department study describes a comprehensive differential response model of thirteen alternatives (Farmer, Michael T., 1981). Four are categories of response by sworn personnel—immediate, expedited, routine and appointment. Immediate response would entail dispatching the beat unit, or nearest available unit, or pulling the nearest unit off a low priority call; expedited response would involve dispatching the nearest unit which is not handling a call; routine means dispatching the beat unit as soon as it is no longer handling a call; and an appointment, as the name implies, is the scheduling of an appointment with the caller. The next four categories are the same types of response by civilian or nonsworn personnel—immediate, expedited, routine, and appointment. The last five are nonmobile responses—telephone, walk-in, mail-in, referral to another agency, and no response. The study suggests the possibility of a matrix relating the type of incident and time of occurrence to these levels of response. Incidents could be allocated into one of eight categories— major personal injury, major property damage/loss, potential personal injury, potential property damage/loss, minor personal injury, minor property damage/loss, other minor crime, and other minor noncrime.

It will be noted that these groupings represent the characteristics of the incident, rather than traditional crime categories. Each of the incidents within each type would be sub-divided on the basis of time of occurrence into one of three subcategories—in progress, proximate, and cold. But the report quickly adds two important cautions. First, there "is certainly nothing sacrosanct about these priority levels. Each police department implementing a differential response model must develop its own dispatch priority levels and definitions of these levels." Second, nothing "can or should replace the good judgment and discretion of operators and dispatchers in ordering a response different from that mandated in the model if the circumstances warrant . . . A highly emotional caller in a relatively minor incident might well call for a different response from what the incident itself warrants (and other examples) . . . Instances where dispatcher decisions are different from the model's prescribed action should be documented with justifications . . . The model should be viewed by dispatchers and complaint operators as a helpful guideline to management's desired choices and not as a strait-jacket" (Farmer, Michael T., 1981).

The principle of the differential police response strategy is also supported by the Management of Police Demand study undertaken by the City of Wilmington, Delaware, Police Department and Public Systems Evaluation (Cahn and Tien, 1981). To what extent can a police agency manipulate or manage the level of calls for service? To what extent can it defer requests for service, and to what extent can it reduce field service?

Traditionally, the demand for police services has been accepted as given, and police administrators have taken it as their task to allocate the corresponding supply to meet the given demand. The Wilmington Management of Demand (MOD) project succeeded in actively managing the demand pattern for police services to achieve an optimal supply pattern. James Tien and Michael Cahn explain (Tien and Cahn, 1980) that three strategies can be used for managing the demand—to decrease the demand level, to diminish demand variance through formally delayed responses, and to provide for less costly or tailored responses through demand screening. Each of these can be addressed by either reactive or proactive means. The Wilmington evaluation was a reactive MOD program. Each noncritical call was treated in one of four ways. It could be formally delayed for up to thirty minutes, with the citizen being advised; it could be handled by telephone, with no further departmental action; the citizen could be asked to walk in to police headquarters; or the caller would be advised that the department would return the call at a prearranged time. Following a six month transition period, the experiment extended from January to September 1979. Some 22.5% of the "Basic" calls for service were "managed"—mainly past larceny, past malicious mischief, past burglary, and added information calls. But, on the basis of citizen surveys, Tien and Cahn estimate that a higher percentage of citizens would be favorably disposed to MOD responses—"perhaps as high as 50 to 60%" (Cahn and Tien, 1981). Surveys of citizens and police personnel suggest satisfaction with the services offered.

PREVENTIVE PATROL

The Kansas City Preventive Patrol Experiment raises critical questions about the utility of a costly and time-consuming police activity, traditional preventive patrol. On the one hand, the study may mean, as noted earlier in Chief Joseph McNamara's words, that "routine patrol in marked police cars has little value in preventing crime or making citizens feel safe" and that many of the resources expended on traditional preventive patrol could be productively reallocated. Traditional or routine preventive patrol in this sense means random driving around a beat in an undirected and unsupervised manner, theoretically exerting a deterrent effect by visible presence, reducing the opportunity for crime by increasing the chances of arrest, and making citizens feel safer.

Less extreme than McNamara's conclusion is Larson's formulation of a positive interpretation of the study's results. If conditions "warrant a change in the spatial deployment of units within a confined region such as a precinct, district, or division, then if procedures are followed that are similar to those used in Kansas City, such redeployments can be made without suffering degradations in service (either actual or perceived) in the depleted regions. In other words, a roll call sergeant or higher level planner could on any given tour of duty assign two or more units to some beats (proactive), one unit to other beats (reactive). Changing crime patterns and other factors affecting public safety would seem to motivate the need for such flexible and focused deployments" (Larson, 1975).

Still another conclusion is that the experiment should be rejected. The methodology of the experiment has been criticized—for example by Davis and Knowles (1975), Larson (1975), Feinberg, Larntz, and Reiss (1976), Zimring (1976), and Schell *et al.* (1976). For instance, Schell *et al.* point out the problems of the location of the cars withdrawn from reactive beats when not responding to calls for service, the small sizes of the beats, and the small sample sizes of the surveys. They point out that "most of what is commonly called 'knowledge' about traditional preventive patrol is, in fact, opinion based primarily on experimental evidence . . . and, as a result, few definitive statements can be made about the impact of alternative approaches to patrol upon the ability of departments to realize the goals of patrol" (Schell *et al.*, 1976).

Fifteen beats were used in the study. Beginning in October 1972, the number of marked police cars was increased by three times in five of these beats (the proactive beats); it was maintained at the same level in five matched (control) beats and preventive patrol was eliminated, apart from that associated with police responding to calls for service, in five other matched (reactive) beats. Victimization, opinion, and reported crime data were analyzed for the year-long duration of the study. "What the experiment found is that the three experimental patrol conditions appeared not to affect crime, service delivery, and citizen feelings in ways the public and the police often assume they do" (Kelling *et al.*, 1974). The technical report of the study gave examples such as the following. As revealed in the victimization surveys, the experimental conditions had no significant effect on residential and nonresidential burglaries, auto thefts, larcenies involving auto accessories, robberies or vandalism—crimes traditionally considered deterable through preventive patrol. As for rates of reporting crime to the police, few differences and no consistent patterns of differences occurred across experimental conditions. Few significant differences and no consistent pattern of differences occurred across experimental conditions in terms of citizen attitudes toward police services. Citizen fear of crime, overall, was not affected by experimental conditions. Experimental conditions did not appear to affect significantly citizen satisfaction with the police as a result of their encounters with police officers.

Certainly, this study cannot be assumed to show that police patrol is of no value—as the Kansas City report itself points out. Further, such a view cannot be reconciled with later studies—for example, that by Schnelle et al. (1977) showing that increases in night patrol coverage had an impact on Part I crimes during a period of saturation patrol, but increases in the day patrol did not—or, for example, the Wilson and Boland (1978) study showing that police patrol strategies such as aggressive patrol affect the robbery rate. Clearly, an interpretation can apply only to the type of traditional patrol activity then used in Kansas City and to the kinds of manpower variations used in the experiment. It does not suggest, for instance, that increasing preventive patrol by twenty (rather than three) times would have had no effect, or that eliminating preventive patrol in the city would not have resulted in severe disorder.

The possible implications of this and other patrol studies were described elsewhere by the present writer in the following terms, and the comment still seems appropriate. "The mixed messages that come from these and other studies (such as Press, 1971; Chaiken et al., 1974, as well as Bright, 1969) may be variously interpreted. One interpretation is that preventive patrol of the level and of the character usually undertaken in U.S. cities has negligible impact on the environment of crime and citizen satisfaction. Another is that, while some forms of preventive patrol are effective for some things, traditional preventive patrol is not effective in all respects. The cop on the corner might deter Toad of Toad Hall (a notorious hot-rodder) but not Willie Sutton (a notorious thief)—or, infractions on the street but not those in private places. Yet another attractive implication is that traditional preventive patrol is an activity out of touch with its environment, and that police agencies can achieve impact if they become more precise—like the surgeon—in their operations" (Farmer, 1980).

Throughout the past decade, some police chiefs have been struggling to find approaches more effective than traditional preventive patrol. Directed patrol was one such approach—and certainly one that has not been adequately developed. Rather than random patrol, directed patrol involves the setting of particular patrol objectives—sometimes by the supervisor in consultation with the officer. The split-force strategy, utilized in the City of Wilmington, is another example. The split-force concept is a method of patrol specialization, based on the separation of the call-for-service response and crime prevention functions of a police patrol force and subsequent assignment of each function to a separately organized group within the patrol force. One part of the patrol force would, barring emergencies, do nothing but respond to calls for service; the other would do nothing but preventive patrol, usually on a directed basis. The formal evaluation of the Wilmington experience concluded that the concept produced an increase in call-for-service response productivity and in the quantity of arrests and clearances (Tien *et al.*, 1979).

In general, alternative approaches to traditional preventive patrol can be classified as either high visibility, low visibility, or community-oriented patrol. High visibility would include variations such as uniformed saturation patrols, aimed at deterrence. Low visibility is directed at arrest and refers to activities like blending and decoy operations (whereby officers dress in street clothes rather than uniforms) or stake-out techniques. Community-oriented patrol, like team policing and the basic car plan, is aimed at identifying the police with a particular area and decentralizing the decision-making.

Police preventive patrol research poses more questions than answers. But preventive patrol continues at a staggering cost in money and in lost crime control opportunities.

CRIMINAL INVESTIGATION

"No area of law enforcement is in greater need of improvement than criminal investigation. The management of criminal investigation, moreover, is less effective on the whole than the management of other police activities." This judgment found in the fourth edition (1977) of O. W. Wilson's and Roy McLaren's *Police Administration*, the standard textbook on the subject, is a testimony to the concern voiced by many police administrators about the character of the investigative function. The statement does not appear in earlier editions.

This concern was fed by the Rand study of the Criminal Investigation Process, a major exploratory effort which undertook a general evaluation of investigative organization and practices (Greenwood *et al.*, 1976). The study described the investigative task and generated hypotheses on how investigators can function more effectively. The study reported six main findings. More than half of all serious reported crime receives no more than superficial attention from investigators. The investigator's time is mainly taken up on cases that experience indicates will not be solved. For solved cases, the investigator spends more time on post-arrest processing rather than the pre-arrest phase. The single most important determinant of whether a case will be solved is the information the victim supplies to the immediately responding patrol officer. Of solved cases in which the offender is not identifiable at the time of the initial report, almost all are cleared as a result of

routine police procedures; and, in many departments, investigators do not thoroughly document the key evidentiary
facts. Despite the criticism that the research went beyond its
data base (see NILECJ, 1977), these conclusions only reinforced the disquiet of many administrators.

At about the same time, the Stanford Research Institute
produced two felony investigation decision models (Greenberg *et al.*, 1973, 1977). Many cases are not investigated by
detectives because the chances of solution are too small, and
the decision not to proceed is generally made on the basis of
"the political clout of the victim(s), the public attention which
is given to the case, and the ad hoc judgments of the investigator" (Farmer, 1976). The decision models were attempts to
provide decision tables for the purpose—"scientific" means
for cutting off unproductive investigations at an early stage.
For example, the decision model for burglary has six information elements (estimated range of time of occurrence, witness' report of offense, on-view report of offense, usable fin-
gerprints, suspect information, and vehicle description) that
are weighted. Only if the score is high enough (higher than
ten) is the case assigned for investigation.

The burglary decision model developed by the Stanford
Research Institute has been extensively tested by the Police
Executive Research Forum in its BIDMOR (Burglary Investigation Decision Model Replication) project (Eck, *et al.*, 1979).
Tested in four Alameda police departments, it indicated an
accuracy range between 57 and 92%. The model was tested by
other groups in Illinois and in Minnesota with accuracy
results of more than 90 and 91–93 percent, respectively. The
Police Executive Research Forum also evaluated the model in
fifteen police departments, concluding that the model is useful for screening cases prior to their assignment to detectives.
The evaluation does recommend, however, that the decision
model not be used without prior testing in the particular setting in which it will be used.

Many police administrators have long been troubled by
the counterproductive but traditional gulf between patrol offi-

cers and investigators. Another study providing information on the investigative function was conducted in the City of Rochester, New York, Police Department (Block and Bell, 1976). This study measured the effectiveness of decentralized patrol/investigator teams assigned to specific areas. It concluded that a police department can probably improve its arrest and clearance rates by assigning detectives to work as part of police teams rather than in traditionally-organized detective units.

Additional information on the nature of the investigative function was provided in another Police Executive Research Forum study, using as study sites Wichita, Kansas; St. Petersburg, Florida; and DeKalb County, Georgia (Eck, 1983). Focusing on the investigation of burglary and robbery, this Forum study reported that "investigations" are not necessarily as wasteful or mismanaged as earlier studies suggested" (Eck, 1983). Detectives and patrol officers were described as contributing equally to the solution of robbery cases. The study concluded that such investigations rarely take more than a total of four hours, spread over as many days. In the quarter of investigations not suspended within two days for lack of leads, the "follow-up work by detectives is a major factor in determining whether suspects will be identified and arrested." However the study pointed out that "detectives and patrol officers alike rely too heavily on victims, who seldom provide information leading to an arrest, and make too little use of those sources of information most likely to lead to arrest—witnesses, informants, their own colleagues, and police records" (Eck, 1983). Accordingly, it offered policy recommendations concerning measures to improve information collection, steps to improve the management of follow-up investigations, and a proposal for an alternative approach to organizing investigations. In preliminary investigations, for example, greater emphasis was urged on collecting physical evidence, on canvassing the neighborhood, on utilizing departmental records, and on using informants. In organization, the report proposed the use of "targeted investigation," an "alternative" problem-solving approach that involves defining problems and selecting targets, planning strategies, conducting investigations, and evaluating performance. "Follow-up investigations, like most other aspects of police work, are dominated by the incoming case flow created by the citizens' reports of offenses," the report explained. Instead of merely investigating incoming cases, the targeted investigation approach is based on having "investigative units attempt to clearly identify the problems with which they are dealing" (Eck, 1983).

The studies, are significant in having made an important beginning in examining the investigative function—of addressing major questions regarding investigator productivity, the management of investigations, and the organization of investigators. Much remains to be studied. But enough is known to give support to the conclusion quoted earlier to the effect that "No area of law enforcement is in greater need of improvement than criminal investigation" (Wilson, 1978).

Nothing less seems required than a new theory, a new perspective, on criminal investigation. The "targeted investigation" approach, advanced in the Forum study (Eck, 1983), suggests one way. The notion of case clearance as the sole objective of detective work seems inadequate; so does the idea that the principal function of the investigator is to solve assigned cases, a view that says little about proactive or police-initiated investigative work. Equally inadequate is the view that the function of a detective is merely to investigate crimes, because this ignores the investigation of suspicious circumstances or individuals. Consider the matter of outcome, for example. It is clear that investigators, like patrol officers, have multiple goals. Besides clearing cases, investigators may pursue other equally important goals to aid citizens—including increasing citizen satisfaction, reducing fear, counseling victims, and deterring further crime. For instance, an investigator cannot consider clearance as the only goal in handling a rape case; increasingly he or she is expected to help the victim cope with her emotional and physical condition and to deal with her sensitively. Outcome as a sole goal is also inadequate because not only does it ignore the means used to achieve the goal; it can actually encourage poor behavior. For example, it is possible to conceive of investigations which result in clearances because they are improperly or corruptly conducted.

SCIENTIFIC AND ANALYTIC CAPABILITY

To date, police agencies have demonstrated only a modest capability in applying scientific and analytic techniques. Great strides have certainly been made since 1968; but, in an increasingly scientific and analytic world, public police agencies can be content with neither their contribution in developing sophisticated techniques nor their capability in applying them. The contribution of public police agencies to innovations in crime prevention has been minor, for instance. The internal capability of police agencies is part of the problem, as well as the absence of a "profit motive." The police service still relies overly on a "paramilitary" career system that, like all such systems, is plagued with difficulties in promoting innovation. But, unlike the military, the police service has not effectively provided for integrating civilians with scientific and analytic skills into the operational decision-making process. Consequently, decisions are not as scientifically sophisticated as they must become some day. The greater use that police agencies can make of scientific and analytical skills in operational management is suggested by experience and research on forensics. A similar case could be made for activities like crime analysis.

Despite Supreme Court decisions urging more extensive use of forensic sciences in criminal investigations, physical evidence is used in only a small number of Part I investigations. Estimates of the use vary (e.g. Benson *et al.*, 1970; Ward, 1971; Parker and Gurgin, 1972; Parker and Peterson, 1972; and Rosenthal and Travnicek, 1974), but it is small. For example, the President's Commission on Law Enforcement and Administration of Justice (Science and Technology Task Force Report, 1967) noted a study of 626 burglaries in which there were "indications of evidence at the scene" in 307 cases; evidence was recovered in only 28 cases. The President's Commission on Crime in the District of Columbia in 1966 reported that only 10% of the Part I crime scenes were processed for evidence. Peterson points out that police departments do not usually process crime scenes for evidence, and that, when they do, the work is either incomplete or unsystematic (Peterson, 1974). At a March 1979 national workshop on "Forensic Science Services and the Administration of Justice," W. Wilson Purdy (then Director of the Dade County Public Safety Department) observed that "there is a general lack of understanding among police executives as to what the forensic sciences can do for them" (Purdy, 1978).

The situation is complicated further by the caliber of forensic services themselves. A proficiency study of a sample (some 205) of crime laboratories throughout the nation, conducted in 1978 by the Forensic Sciences Foundation, indicated serious deficiencies in laboratory performance. Participating laboratories were sent samples of common forensic items such as hair, blood, and paint chips. The number of identification errors that were made was high. Among the higher error percentages, for example, were 71.2% (blood), 67.8% (hair), 34% (wood), and 28.2% (firearms). With some reserve, the report observed that "there are several physical types (with) which crime laboratories are having serious difficulties" (Peterson, 1979).

Parallel cases could be made in areas such as resources allocation modeling and crime analysis. Considerable effort has been invested in developing resource allocation capability. Such sophisticated techniques have had only marginal impact on general police practice. Part of the fault has resided in the misunderstanding of the researchers, as is demonstrated later. For instance, efforts to reduce average response time turned out (as demonstrated in the Kansas City Response Time Study) to be a type of chimera; on the technical level, the objective was inappropriate. Next, the models were not intended to provide for the reality that resource allocation is not entirely a technical matter for the police administrator, who, after all, operates within a political context. Practitioners have been somewhat remiss as well—for failing to understand and to demand more from the researchers. Microcomputer capability may help bridge this gap for practitioners, because it provides hands-on and easy-to-use personal computing capacity for administrators.

The crime analysis case differs from that of resources allocation in that no significant technical advances have been sought during the period; rather, crime analysis has been a matter of applying relatively straightforward techniques to crime data maintained in police agencies. An overall description of police crime analysis programs is provided in Reinier, 1977. Like resource allocation, crime analysis has neither reached its full potential nor has its impact been felt by police agencies.

IMPLICATIONS

Police agencies can make better use of their police resources. The research findings described in this chapter have not only made this clear, they have suggested the shape of the changes needed. There really is a possibility of a revolution throughout the entire range of police operational practices. The change needed is appropriately described as revolutionary in that (at a minimum) substantial adjustment seems desirable in the management of field operations like patrol and criminal investigations, where traditional approaches appear inadequate. But it is appreciated that police institutions, like other bureaucracies, operate within a variety of programmatic, political, and other constraints. "Possible" revolutions need never happen. Rather, it is likely that changes will evolve over time and that prevailing practices will be overturned slowly.

Further tinkering with the professional model is conceivable in responding to the challenges of these research results. Considerable gains can be expected from such adjustments, and they are clearly valuable. But the real benefits of the cumulative lessons of these studies can be realized, it seems, only through advancing to the next step. This next step is the development of a new form of police institution.

CHAPTER 3

The Art of Policing

To achieve results in police policy-making and administration, no less than in areas like medicine, science is invaluable but insufficient: art is needed. Faced with the need for solutions workable now in a particular location, the police practitioner is often disappointed by scientific or research results such as those discussed in the previous chapter. If so, he expects too much from them. Research usually offers the practitioner limited information about limited propositions. The information is limited in that the conclusions can be no more than probable and tentative. The Kansas City Preventive Patrol Study, for example, cannot offer certainty about the value of preventive patrol. In a world where the only scientific certainty is that there is no certitude, even a thousand replications cannot give more than greater probability. Research propositions are limited in that they usually speak to only a part of the practitioner's problem. That rapid response time is unimportant in most police situations is important; but it is partial information for the practitioner surrounded by the complex plethora of problems associated with his particular patrol management situation. No matter how much the "science" of medicine develops, the "art" of the physician is essential at least in reconciling the needs of the patient and in tailoring the science to the complexities of the particular case. Similarly, the art of the police manager will always be required in working toward the ideal of the new form of police agency. Absent a police science as developed as medical science, the need for the practitioner's art may well be greater in the police situation.

The art of the police policy-maker and administrator is to move the police institution toward the new form. The policy-making and management art required for effective movement must be developed in view of the circumstances of the case, both the situation of the agency and of the administrator himself. The police practitioner must start, for example, with the condition of the agency—just as the physician starts with the patient's situation. The grossly underdeveloped or severely ill patient cannot usually be transformed overnight into a marathon runner. So, too, the police institution without professional practices and personnel cannot typically be reformed at one stroke into the new form of police agency. A gradualist approach is usually more practical. This involves pushing in this direction one moment, pulling in that the next—striving for limited gains, but always aiming (although with conscious detours, starts and stops) toward the goal of the new form of agency. The police practitioner, perhaps less than the physician, must also be conscious of his own situation—the opportunities and the limitations of his policy-making and managerial discretion within the police, political, programmatic, and other environments of which he is a part.

This chapter continues with the diagnosis of the problem, providing information on the substance of the new form of police agency toward which the practitioner should move. The contention is made that currently police agencies, despite their action orientation, are essentially directed toward process and that there is insufficient emphasis on the definition of purpose. This contention is addressed in two sections. The first borrows from the same 1981 article by the writer in *Police*

Studies (Farmer, 1981) and comments on the issue of ends and means in policing. It shows the shift in thinking that has recently occurred and indicates the delicate balancing act required of the management artist. The second offers a case study of dedication to process—that of police resources allocation decision-making. This chapter, then, lays a foundation for the discussion in Chapter 5 of police purposes.

ENDS AND MEANS IN POLICING

Herman Goldstein has done a great service for the police community by emphasizing that law enforcement has devoted disproportionate attention to means rather than ends. His comment, quoted in Chapter 1, deserves repetition—that "the whole reform movement in policing has been short-sighted in focusing almost exclusively on improving the police establishment without having given adequate attention to some serious underlying problems that grow out of the basic arrangements for policing in our society" (Goldstein, 1977). In 1979, he again stressed the importance of substance rather than mere efficiency (Goldstein, 1979).

The bulk of research studies have focused on matters of internal institutional efficiency; examples are most of the studies (noted in the previous chapter) on operations management and overall administration. Such studies are clearly significant. But more attention is needed to outputs—to consideration of the results and end-products of policing. It is likely that this attention to ends, rather than means, will gain force in coming years. The most persuasive argument advanced for this contention is the growth of consumer orientation, a trend that Goldstein argues has not yet been felt fully by policing. Among the other reasons are the financial problems (the Proposition 13 feelings) now widespread, resistance felt toward organizational change, and the fact that the effectiveness of even the best and most efficient police agencies is being questioned.

The present concern over ends and means has come late to policing, although the writer is not suggesting that the topic has never before been discussed. Thus it is possible for the police research community to put the matter in better perspective by examining experience elsewhere. American Public Administration has focused on the problem since at least the late forties when the First Hoover Commission (1947–1949) popularized the notion and practice of performance budgeting. Owing much to the rising decisional technologies such as Economics and Systems Analysis, this new approach to budgeting eventually took the more defined form of the Program Performance Budgeting System (PPBS)—introduced in 1961 in the Department of Defense, extended throughout the Federal Government in 1965, and losing favor by 1971. As the approach evolved into a strategy, it was not only a marriage between program planning and budgeting but also a movement from program accounting to results area analysis—from means to ends.

This concern for results area analysis in the Federal administration survived the death of PPBS, and emerged in another form under former President Richard M. Nixon as Management-by-Objectives, a term coined by Peter Drucker. This approach differed from PPBS because it operated from the lowest level upward; it worked mainly on an intra-agency basis, and it had more flexibility. But it was essentially the same as PPBS in concentrating on ends, as was its successor Zero-Based Budgeting (ZBB). Introduced in 1977, and deriving from Peter Pyhrr, ZBB again differs in detail. For instance, PPBS was centralizing and MBO was decentralizing; ZBB has elements of both tendencies. But like its predecessors, ZBB emphasizes ends and not means.

During this extensive history, a debate occurred over concentrating on ends and means in budgeting. Prominent among the champions of PPBS were James Schlesinger and Charles Schultze. As Schlesinger explained in testimony to the Jackson Subcommittee of the Senate, PPBS offered several advantages: namely, avoiding simple statements of noble purpose, analyzing outputs and not just inputs, designing systems with realistic budgetary limits, and taking long-run costs into account. Schultze, in his testimony, noted that PPBS is the key to forcing agencies to look at objectives, to quantify, to measure costs, and to analyze alternatives. On the other side were the incrementalists like Aaron Wildawsky and Charles Lindblom. Among the reasons advanced by Wildawsky for favoring incrementalism is that "the best you can get is better than the perfection you can't get." Lindblom advocated Disjointed Incrementalism (Lindblom, 1959). Noting that nonincremental proposals are typically politically irrelevant, he argued that administrators should seek agreement on means rather than ends. The distinction between policy and programs (ends and means) is not meaningful, he argued, and he observed that "it is easier to agree on plans with built-in policy goals." Rather than a rational and comprehensive (or root) approach, he favored a method of successive limited (branch) comparisons. This long controversy has clear relevance for the recent attention on output in police research. In summary, neither approach (concentrating on either ends or means) has all of the arguments on its side.

Among the output-focused studies that are significant are Herman Goldstein's work on Problem Focused Policing. Rather than merely dealing with a succession of incidents (e.g., calls for service), Goldstein argues that police agencies should focus on coping with overall output problems. He defines the police job as dealing with such problems. Working with the Madison and other police departments, he has attempted to add flesh to his concept. As a starting point, he believes that police agencies need to give greater specificity and more depth in identifying and delineating the problem— relying less on mere crime categories, for instance.

Following problem identification and research, Goldstein explains how a police agency has a much wider range of alternatives than those traditionally utilized. The possible alternative responses are described in Goldstein's 1979 article, a gripping illustration of how process-bound and limited so

much of the police response remains. Without doubt, Goldstein's work is a landmark in police research, of significance
for other countries besides the United States. However, out-
put-oriented studies are neither new nor limited to this one
study.

This emphasis on output is a valuable corrective to the
earlier focus in police research (an emphasis that is natural in
a developing area) on means. The latest trend represents a logical growth in the study of police matters and offers ample
research opportunities. Of course, it must be conceded that
terms like "ends" and "means" do present semantic problems.
Just as every system is embedded in other larger systems, so
an "end" is likely to be the "means" to yet another "end"—
and so on. But the semantic problem does not destroy the utility of the distinction. Herbert Simon observed in his classic
work on Administrative Behavior (Simon, 1945) that the organization should be focused on the operator, and Egon Bittner
has repeatedly observed how we have failed to give adequate
attention to the craft of policing—an end-product of the
police institution. Bittner draws an analogy with medicine,
asking whether hospitals have improved over the past two
centuries as a result of interest in hospital administration or
of advances in the practices of medicine. "For me, the work of
the 'cop on the beat' has always made up 95 percent of the
picture. The rest stands to policing like hospital administration stands to medicine," wrote Bittner in a 1978 letter. Police
institutions, like other organizational entities, have at least
two sets of outputs—the corporate output and the individual
operative's work. At the corporate level, an output may be the
translation into practice of a decision to allocate specific
resources in a particular way to cope with a problem (e.g.,
enforcement of Blue Law violations in a particular way). At
the individual operative level, in the police situation, there is
the craft of order maintenance. Certainly, there have been
studies—both anecdotal and systematic—of police officer
activity. Jonathan Rubinstein's *City Police* (Rubinstein, 1973) is
thought by many to be among the best. But, as Egon Bittner

has pointed out, there is an opportunity for systematic analysis and improvement of the substance of good police street work. This recognizes the reality that "good" police officers have developed special knowledge, judgment, and skills in handling police situations—capabilities that may be operationalized, analyzed, strengthened, and taught to other officers.

TRIUMPH OF MEANS OVER ENDS

This section describes an example of how police resources allocation decision-making techniques have been developed without appropriate reference to definition of purpose. One reason for this triumph of means over ends is the difficulty of measuring ultimate outputs. Another reason is that it permits the "ugly" reality of the political environment of police management to be ignored. For these reasons, intermediate outputs were selected to serve as the foundation for resource allocation techniques. But the structure will surely collapse when the truth becomes more widely appreciated that the intermediate outputs are essentially unimportant to the police purpose. The major legacy of this investment of intellectual and financial resources in the development of such allocation techniques has been a moral. The moral is that purpose and not process should be the goal.

To this end, the following describes and assesses the practice and literature of police resources allocation decision-making. This is done in three parts. The first discusses proportional distribution techniques. The second outlines the mathematical modelling approaches. The third reports on a survey of police resources allocation decision-making practice.

Police resources allocation, it has been explained, is viewed in practice and in the literature as the narrow, technical problem of determining how manpower is to be assigned among alternative geographical areas (e.g., central city, suburb, poor area, rich area) and alternative functions

(e.g., preventing crime, apprehending criminals). The allocation process is treated in the criminal justice literature as an
apolitical matter, an administrative issue to be determined on
a "professional" or "technical" basis. Literature and research,
in this spirit, have focused on two major areas of inquiry. The
first has been to develop proportional distribution techniques,
with the objectives of equalizing among geographical sub-
units either police workload (using workload formulae) or the
provision of police protective services (through hazard formulae). The second has been in the application of mathematical (or computer) modelling to manpower allocation problems. These are described below under the first and second
subparts.

Under the third subpart, selected results are reported
from a survey of police agencies in U.S. cities with populations over 100,000 and of police departments in Virginia communities with populations over 5,000 (Farmer, 1981). This survey shows that the characterization of the police resources
allocation process in the criminal justice literature is insufficient. The characterization essentially constitutes a special
case where political considerations do not affect the technical
decision-making. The survey data provide evidence that a politics–administration dichotomy does not obtain in police
resources allocation, a conclusion to be expected in view of the
consensus in contemporary Public Administration literature
on the topic (e.g., see Morrow, 1980). Further, they show that
other characteristics of the allocation process also differ from
those implied in the literature.

Proportional Distribution Techniques

Proportional distribution techniques constitute the
approach most widely used for police resources allocation
decision-making. In the survey described in the third subsection below, some 58 percent of the large U.S. police agencies
reported utilizing workload/hazard formulae. The objective
of such techniques is to equalize either police workload

(workload formulae) or the need for police protection services (hazard formulae) among geographical areas such as commands, districts, or beats. Both methods involve identifying and weighting factors considered relevant for manpower allocation. Factors usually include measures of crime rate (e.g., number of Part 1 or 2 crimes), measures of police activity (e.g., number of calls for service), and measures of indirect demand for police service (e.g., number of street miles to be patrolled). If a workload formula is utilized, the weightings represent the man-hours required to cope with each factor. In the case of a hazard formula, the weightings reflect the relative significance of each factor in terms of the need for police protective service. Police manpower is assigned on a proportional basis, with the total manpower available being allocated in proportion to the relative sizes of the workload or hazard indices (products of the respective formulae) in each geographical command.

Kakalik and Wildhorn give examples of hazard formulae used in two cities (Kakalik and Wildhorn, *Aids to Decision-Making in Police Patrol*, 1971). One city utilizes equal weightings and employs the following factors occurring in the specified districts—percent of city's Part I crimes, percent of city's Part 2 crimes, percent of city's custody arrests, percent of city's injury accidents, percent of city's ambulance runs, percent of city's fires, percent of city's police "services" rendered, percent of city's population, percent of city's population density, percent of city's area, percent of city's road miles, percent of city's licensed premises, percent of city's store doors, and percent of city's schools. The second city utilizes the following factors in manning the designated district, with the weightings indicated in parentheses—percent of city's selected crimes and attempts (5), percent of city's radio calls handled by radio car (4), percent of city's felony arrests (3), percent of city's misdemeanor arrests (1), percent of city's property loss (1), percent of city's injury traffic accidents (1), percent of city's vehicles recovered (1), percent of city's population (1), percent of city's street miles (1), and percent of city's population density (1).

Some jurisdictions do undertake time studies to assist in determining weightings (e.g., see Public Administration Service, 1969). But, essentially, factors and the weightings of both workload and hazard formulae are subjectively chosen, and they vary among jurisdictions. Weights typically range from 4 to 5 for serious crimes and from 1 to 3 for miscellaneous police services and radio calls; in some instances, all factors are accorded equal weights (see Kakalik and Wildhorn, *Aids to Decision-Making in Police Patrol,* 1971). Factors chosen also vary in number and kind (e.g., see O. W. Wilson, 1977).

August Vollmer is reported to have utilized proportional workload as the basis for assigning the Berkeley, California, police strength as early as 1909 (Chapman, 1970). But the practice developed only slowly. Thus in 1931 the Wickersham Commission can comment that, "The statistics section is rarely the effective tool in police work into which it can be made. Executives in general have not appreciated the strategic value of the vast amount of information which lies dormant around police departments" (Wickersham Commission, 1931, pp. 106–107).

As late as 1958, Frank Walton could report that " . . . the assignment of police manpower in relation to police problems, in terms of day of week, time of day and area . . . is by no means widespread" (Walton, 1970, p. 297). By the mid-1960's the notion had become widely established (Reinier, :977).

In the United States, the development of the proportional distribution approach based on the use of hazard and workload formulae owes much not only to August Vollmer but also to Orlando W. Wilson. Contributions were made also by others such as Elmer Graper, Raymond B. Fosdick, and Bruce Smith (Chapman, 1970, p. 292). In addition to being the first police chief executive to have utilized beat analysis, Vollmer was the principal architect of the Wickersham Commission's *Report on the Police* which recommended that police records should be used in the development of strategic plans (Wickersham Commission, 1931, p. 39). In a 1933 speech, Vollmer explained his thoughts on patrol allocation based on analysis of police records. "On the assumption of regularity of crime and similar occurrences it is possible to tabulate those occurrences by areas within a city and thus determine the points which have the greatest danger of such crimes and what points have the least danger" (Chapman, 1970). But it was O. W. Wilson who developed and popularized the use of hazard and workload formulae, specifying the factors to be considered and their relative weights in 1941 in his influential publication, *Distribution of Police Patrol Force* (Wilson, 1941). Wilson also repeated his views in his widely used textbook *Police Administration*, which appeared first in 1950 and then in revised editions in 1963, 1972, and 1977.

The experience of the New York City Police Department, illustrating the introduction and use in a large department of proportional manpower deployment based on a hazard formula, was noted in Chapter 1. Prior to 1955, New York depended completely on command discretion, a method relying entirely on commanders' experience and knowledge. Describing "command discretion," Kakalik commented that, "In some large departments no formalized quantitative procedures are employed either to substantiate requests for changes in police force size or to aid in deploying men to duty tours and patrol districts" (Kakalik *et al.* *(Aids to Decision-Making in Police Patrol)*, 1971). Some 11 percent of the departments in the National Sample of police agencies serving U.S. populations greater than 100,000 still report reliance on this method.

In 1955, the New York City Police Department introduced what is called a Post Hazard Plan (see New York City Police Department, *Rules and Procedures*, Chapter 18, Paragraph 82.0). This plan provided for nine factors and contemplated updating the allocations on a five-year basis:

Crimes of violence	25%
Other crimes and offenses	20

Juvenile delinquency	15
Accident and aided cases	10
Population (permanent and transient)	10
Area	5
Business establishments	5
School crossings, park areas, playgrounds and permanent recreation areas	5
Radio alarms transmitted	5

With only minor modifications and despite dissatisfaction, this Post Hazard Plan has remained in effect until the present day.

The workload/hazard method has the advantage over the command discretion approach that allocation decisions are made following an analysis (however imperfect) of explicit criteria. The use of "explicit" criteria facilitates the establishment of patrol priorities (e.g., emphasis on street crime by appropriate weighting of this factor), thus permitting commanders more direction and control over the emphasis of law enforcement practice in their jurisdiction.

The weaknesses of the approach have also been widely discussed. It has been pointed out, for example, that a workload formula "equalizes the workload of patrol units, without regard to any other measures of patrol performance" (Chaiken, 1975, p. 28). The Rand report concludes, "Thus, it is possible for two geographical commands which are nearly identical in all respects other than size to obtain allocations that result in substantially different queuing delays for calls for service, travel times, patrol frequencies, and other measures of performance" (Chaiken, 1975, p. 28). As Ferrara has shown, disparities can be predicted (Ferrara, 1975). The significance of such factors as queuing delays, travel times, and patrol frequencies is, however, another issue.

The defects of hazard/workload formulae are also discussed by Richard Larson. "The inherently linear form of a hazard formula precludes description of the highly nonlinear and complex interactions among system components that are often seen, for example, in police systems. Such a formula also attempts an overly simple deterministic depiction of a system in which many of the variables are probabilistic and often highly interdependent" (Larson, 1972, p. 38). And Larson later adds that a hazard formula "does not provide a police administrator with such policy-relevant information as the response time of the patrol force, or the probability that a patrol car will intercept a crime in progress, or any of a number of other operational quantities" (Larson, 1972, pp. 38–39).

Both Chaiken and Larson go further, asserting that hazard formulae lead to distorted results. For example, Chaiken indicates that in many situations the higher the weight given to a specified category of crimes in the hazard formula (violent outside crimes, for example), the smaller will be the number of officers assigned by the hazard formula (Chaiken, 1975, p. 29). "As a result, by increasing the weight for violent outside crimes, the administrator in the example city brings about an allocation that increases the fraction of time that officers in high crime commands spend on unimportant incidents" (Chaiken, 1975, p. 30).

Larson points out that because the number of arrests and reported crimes depend partly on the number of police officers allocated to an area, a hazard formula may indicate a need for more personnel in areas already relatively over-allocated. As he states, "Crime suspects are more likely to be apprehended in an area that is sufficiently staffed than in one with overworked or saturated resources" (Larson, 1972, p. 39).

Larson also notes what he considers to be the unsatisfactory character of workload/hazard formulae in allocating officers for preventive patrol services. Police patrol activities can be viewed as consisting of either coping with incidents or undertaking preventive patrol. The former are the activities involved in responding to crime and service calls from the public and in handling incidents encountered by the police officer; the latter are activities designed to deter crime and disorderly behavior through "police omnipresence," to intercept criminal activities and to provide a feeling of safety and satisfaction in the community (For discussion, see Chapman, 1970). Typically, cities determine the level of preventive patrol effort on a residual basis, treating preventive patrol as the time left over after other duties are performed. As Larson indicates, this "can have the perverse effect of providing most patrol during the least busy hours and least patrol during busiest hours" (Larson, 1972, p. 131). And he adds, "While the desired nature of the relationship between call-for-service activity and preventive patrol activity is not known, it would be very surprising if more preventive patrol is consistently required when fewer calls for service are received" (Larson, 1972, pp. 131–132).

Mathematical Modeling

Computer-based methods are utilized by a significant minority of U.S. police agencies. In the survey noted below, some 31 percent in the national and 16 percent in the Virginia samples reported using computer-based methods—either Pecam, Hypercube, mini-computer, or other. Significant work in the development of "mathematical modeling" approaches to police manpower allocation has occurred since 1967.

Encouraged largely by the 1967 President's Commission on Law Enforcement and Administration of Justice and by the 1968 Omnibus Crime Control and Safe Streets Act, this work has been carried forward principally by operations research personnel at the Massachusetts Institute of Technology and the Rand Corporation. Commented the President's Commission, "The most effective way of deploying and employing a department's patrol force is a subject about which deplorably little is known . . . This sort of research has scarcely begun in America, partly because few police departments have the funds or the personnel to devise, develop, and test innovative procedures" (President's Commission, 1967, p. 65). With the Federal funds made available under the Omnibus Crime Control and Safe Streets Act, operations research groups and activities were initiated in a few of the larger police departments.

For example, an operations research task force was established in 1968 under Albert H. Bottoms in the City of Chicago Police Department, and it produced its report *Allocation of Resources in the Chicago Police Department* in November 1969 (Bottoms, 1969). This task force developed a computer simulation of the communications process, paid particular attention to robbery, and experimented with split force patrol; but lasting results did not materialize. (For a general account of this project, see Bottoms, Albert H., and Nilsson, Ernst K., "Operations Research," *Police Chief*, May 1970, pp. 22–26.)

Another operations research group was established in the St. Louis, Missouri, Police Department. The St. Louis project developed a resources allocation program, which formed the basis of Law Enforcement Manpower Resource Allocation System (LEMRAS) (see McEwan, 1966). LEMRAS, developed by the International Business Machines (IBM) corporation, utilized exponential smoothing to estimate future call rates and service times from past data. It also calculated queue delay (the time between the receipt of a call from a citizen at the police communications center and the dispatch of a responding police vehicle) in terms of the number of patrol units on duty. LEMRAS users could then establish performance standards for queue delay, and thus calculate patrol car assignments geographically and chronologically to meet the standards.

The most significant work on the "mathematical modeling" approach toward police resources allocation has been conducted, as was indicated above, at the Massachusetts Institute of Technology (MIT) and at the Rand Corporation. The MIT activity has been undertaken by, or under the leadership of, Richard C. Larson, who has worked both at MIT and at the New York City Rand Corporation. Larson's book, *Urban Police Patrol Analysis*, describes some of this work (Larson, 1972). Virtually all of the computer models developed for police allocation purposes have been directed at patrol needs. Four main types have been distinguished by Chaiken (Chaiken *et al.*, 1976). (Excluded from consideration are the manpower scheduling models, which can be used to determine schedules of working and off-duty days for individual patrol and other police officers). First there are patrol car allocation models, analytic models that are intended to specify the number of patrol units that should be on duty at various times and various geographical points in the jurisdictions. These patrol car allocation models are intended to address issues such as the allocation of patrol force among geographical areas; the number of officers required per shift; and the hours of shifts. A variant form is the analytical model that estimates queuing delays under the assumption that patrol car strength varies over time; this is usually called the dynamic queuing model.

Second are the simulation models which facilitate the analysis of patrol policy issues. Simulation models, reflecting more details of a system than do analytical models, represent the operations of a system to reproduce the same statistical behavior as is found in "reality." Always descriptive rather than prescribing the best solution as would an analytical optimization model, simulations let the user know "what would happen if" he made this or that decision. Examples of police patrol issues which can be addressed by simulation models are the effects of functional specialization among patrol cars; the "value" of an automated vehicle locator system; and the consequences of changing dispatching rules.

Third, there are the analytical models developed to assist in the design of patrol car beat boundaries. These models calculate a variety of performance measures (such as travel time) for each beat design, and permit the user to see the effects of alternate beat patterns on these measures.

In a fourth category is the linear programming optimization model that minimizes patrol tours required within the constraint of a user-specified car requirement for each hour. Outputs are data such as the best times to start shifts and to take rest breaks, and the best number of patrol units to be used per shift.

Each of these four categories of model is now discussed briefly in turn. In describing the models in these categories, liberal references have been made to Chaiken. His book, *Crim-*

inal Justice Models: An Overview, provides an outstanding summary of technical information on police and other criminal justice mathematical models (Chaiken *et al.*, 1976).

Most of the patrol car allocation models (as Chaiken observes) are based on the system developed at the St. Louis Department or a program designed by Richard Larson. LEMRAS, it has already been noted, is an example of the former derivation. Examples of the latter are the programs developed by Urban Sciences (Urban Sciences, 1972) by Richard Mudge (Mudge, 1974) and at UCLA (UCLA, 1974). Chaiken explains that the two main features of the St. Louis system were prediction and queuing. It was noted earlier that the St. Louis system involved predicting the number of calls to occur in each hour of the week in each small segment (or Pauly Area) into which the city was divided. Then, given the number of police cars in the field, "it was possible to predict the percentage of callers who will experience a queuing delay"—a delay between the time the call for service reaches the police dispatcher and the time when the dispatcher assigns a police car to respond to the call. Department policy was (Chaiken notes) that this percentage should not exceed 15, and this then determined the number of patrol cars needed. The LEMRAS program did contain some advances: for instance, it operated on the assumption that all priority 1 calls would be assigned before priority 2 calls, and so on. Nevertheless, it was basically similar to the St. Louis system.

The most important advance of Larson's program over LEMRAS, as Chaiken notes, was consideration of performance measures other than queuing delay. (Another significant advance was the capability of allocating a fixed number of patrol cars. This reflects the reality that, in the short run, this number is relatively inflexible). Larson's program, as Chaiken explains, included consideration of three additional performance measures—workload, travel time, and preventive patrol frequency (number of times any point in the beat is passed by a patrol car). This advance was important in that queue delay cannot be a satisfactory sole performance criterion. Larson's program was tested but never utilized by the New York City Police Department; however, the Rotterdam Police Department wrote and implemented its own version of the Larson program (McEwan and Larson, 1974). The Urban Sciences, Richard Mudge, and UCLA programs represent, according to Chaiken, no significant conceptual advances over Larson's work, and have also encountered little user acceptance. Mudge's program does return to the St. Louis approach, however, in seeking to field enough cars to keep queue delays below specified limits. A more powerful program, Patrol Car Allocation Model, was developed in 1975 by the Rand Corporation on the basis of Larson's program as improved by Mudge. It incorporates most of the features of previous programs (Chaiken and Dormont, 1975).

The performance measures utilized by these programs are limited to factors such as workload, travel time, preventive patrol frequency, and queuing delay. This is illustrated by reviewing Chaiken's description (Chaiken *et al.*, 1976) of the output of the Patrol Car Allocation Model when it is operating in descriptive mode. Information displayed includes "the number of cars assigned to each command at each time of the day; information about patrol car workloads; information about the amount of preventive patrol done by the patrol cars; the average length of time from the dispatch of a patrol car until its arrival at the scene of an incident; the percentage of calls that have to wait in queue until a patrol car is available for dispatch to the incident; the average length of time that calls of various priorities have to wait in queue; and the average total response time (time in queue plus travel time)" (Chaiken *et al.*, 1976). Chaiken commented elsewhere on this list as follows. "These capabilities are about the best that can be accomplished at the present time. PCAM (Patrol Car Allocation Model) permits a department to specify its objectives and then to find allocations of patrol units that meet these objectives. To the extent that performance measures of importance to police administrators (e.g., deterrence of crime, apprehension of criminal offenders) are omitted from the program, it is not because they are deemed unimportant, but rather because there is no known way to estimate them" (Chaiken, 1975, p. 35).

The second category of model (as outlined above) is the simulation model used to examine the effects of systems changes without incurring the cost, disruption, and time disadvantage of making changes in the real world. As pointed out by Chaiken (Chaiken *et al.*, 1976), police patrol simulation models are used to analyze policy issues such as the effects on response time and workload of increasing or decreasing the number of patrol units; beat sector design; the effect of various dispatching rules on workload and response time; and the effects of other modes of patrol (e.g., helicopters) on patrol car workload. Such models have been developed by the Brooklyn Polytechnic Institute for the New York City Police Department (Hauser, 1969), by the Illinois Institute of Technology for the Aurora Police Department (Smith, 1973), by Richard C. Larson for the Boston Police Department (Urban Sciences, 1971) and by the New York City Rand Institute for the New York City Police Department (Kolesar and Walker, 1975). None of the models served other than for experimental purposes. All have significant limitations in reflecting or "simulating" the real world (Chaiken *et al.*, 1976).

The Hauser model developed in 1969 at the Polytechnic Institute of Brooklyn for the New York City Police Department was described as extremely limited, for example. It recorded neither the location of incidents nor the identity of patrol units assigned jobs. Thus it was essentially "modelling a standard multi-serving queuing system with indistinguishable servers" (Chaiken *et al.*, 1976). It could provide response time data and information such as the average number of busy patrol cars. But it could neither measure individual workloads nor calculate average travel times, nor design patrol beats, nor investigate the effects of various dispatching rules. As another example, Larson developed a more powerful general police patrol model, and this was reprogrammed and adapted by Urban Sciences Incorporated in 1971 for the Boston Police

Department. Among the limitations of that model were that it made no provision for variations in the rate of arrival of calls for service (the calls were generated internally), for meal breaks, for inter-precinct dispatches, for dispatcher delay, for more than one mode of patrol unit, or for changes in the geometry of the patrol system (Chaiken *et al.*, 1976).

The third category of model outlined above is the beat design model, the analytical model utilized to determine the geographical areas which will be covered by each patrol car. They are used to map beat boundaries with such objectives in mind as balancing inter-unit workloads, equalizing response time, and minimizing the dispatching of patrol units outside assigned sub-areas (Chaiken *et al.*, 1976). Two major beat design models have been developed—Richard Larson's Hypercube Queuing Model (Larson, 1975) and Deepak Bammi's model (Bammi, 1972). Both models have been verified and validated, and the former has been implemented in Boston, Quincy, and Arlington, Massachusetts, and the latter has been implemented in Aurora, Illinois. The differences between the models are relatively minor.

A variant of the patrol car allocation models discussed by Chaiken is the dynamic queuing model developed in 1973 by the Rand Corporation for (but never implemented in) the New York City Police Department (Kolesar and Walker, 1975). The 1973 model was entirely descriptive, but a 1974 version prescribed the minimum hourly patrol car requirements needed to provide a specified level of service. The distinguishing feature of this dynamic queuing model is that it provides for variations in time in the rate of calls for service and in the number of patrol cars. In descriptive mode, the major issues addressed by such a model are those related to time—e.g., are there periods of the day when the probability of a queuing delay is usually high?

A linear programming model was developed in 1974 by the Rand Institute for the New York City Police Department to assist in achieving a specified number of cars on duty while consuming the smallest possible number of car hours (Kolesar *et al.*, 1974). Among the policy issues addressed (as noted in Chaiken *et al.*, 1976) are the best times for scheduling tours; the optimum times for meal breaks; and the relationship of the number of car tours to various service levels. Limitations include the fact that the model is not constrained by the available level of resources (it cannot be used to determine the best allocation of a given number of cars) and the fact that service level is defined in terms of hourly car requirements.

The performance measures utilized hitherto by the "mathematical model" builders can be characterized as intermediate performance indicators—in the sense that they measure activities or goals deemed important in achieving larger activities or goals. Reliance is placed not on fundamental goals such as crime deterrence or apprehension of criminals. Rather, it is placed on subordinate activities or goals considered significant, not as ends in themselves, but as means to much larger goals. Thus, Chaiken's comment (pp. 72–73) requires reemphasis—"To the extent that performance measures of importance to police administrators (e.g., deterrence of crime, apprehension of criminal offenders) are omitted from the program, it is not because they are deemed unimportant but rather because there is no known way to estimate them" (Chaiken, 1975). Particular emphasis is placed by the model builders on response time—with variants on this notion such as the length of time calls remain in various queues. Lesser indicators used include preventive patrol frequency and workload.

The adequacy of utilizing response time as a major criterion in resources allocation is questioned (by implication) by the results of the Response Time Study conducted by the Kansas City Police Department (Bieck *et al.*, 1977, 1979, 1980). The study, it was noted in Chapter 2, indicates that response time (the time between the dispatch of a police car and the arrival of the car at the scene of the incident) is not as significant a factor as is traditionally assumed because the time between the occurrence of the incident and the moment when it is reported to the police is so much greater. For commercial robbery in Kansas City, for instance, the median time between car dispatch and arrival was found to be 6 minutes and 54 seconds, while the median time between occurrence and reporting was 51 minutes and 18 seconds. For burglaries the data were 6 minutes 15 seconds and 34 minutes 2 seconds, respectively; for larcenies the data were 4 minutes 41 seconds and 54 minutes 40 seconds, respectively; and for auto theft, they were (respectively) 4 minutes 32 seconds and 32 minutes 17 seconds. The consequence of the Kansas City study and its replication (in Jackson-Duvall, San Diego, and Peoria) is that the basic underpinning—response time—of the model builders appears extremely dubious. A principal assumption of the models—the importance of police response time—has been significantly questioned. As Bieck expressed it in his 1980 report, "[B]ecause of the time citizens take to report crimes, police response time will have negligible impact on crime outcomes."

Resource Allocation Practice

What are some of the realities of resource allocation practice? Let us turn to the Police Resources Allocation Decision-Making Survey of U.S. cities with populations over 100,000 (the data from that being referenced as the National Sample) and of Virginia communities over 5,000 in population (that segment being called the Virginia Sample). Specifics of the methodology of this Resources Allocation Survey were presented in Chapter 1 (Farmer, 1981).

A principal survey finding, that "political" or nontechnical factors may well be significant considerations in the resources allocation decision-making of a substantial number of U.S. police agencies, is itemized in the next chapter. Here the focus is on the other findings.

Critical characteristics of the police resources allocation decision-making process are more complex than the criminal justice literature (referenced earlier) implies. This conclusion, supported by the data from the survey, permits the assessment that the criminal justice literature is deficient in major aspects in describing the allocation process. Three differences between the depiction of the process in the present survey and that in the literature are noted in the following paragraphs. First, the following paragraphs report that the survey shows the process to be multilayered, involving layers of interacting decision-makers rather than a single resource allocator. Sometimes the agency head does not know the final dispositions; sometimes the public is also shielded from actual allocations by such means as phantom allocations. Second, the process is shown to be essentially marginal, a matter more of frequent and minor adjustments rather than periodic major redeployments. Third, the process is indicated to involve both functional as well as geographic dimensions. These characteristics are critical in the sense that resource allocation techniques are likely to be more effective if they are designed around the process they are intended to facilitate.

Proportional distribution techniques make up the principal, but certainly not the universal, approach used for resources allocation. Some 58 percent in the National, but only 31 percent in the Virginia, sample reported utilizing hazard/workload formulae. This included some very large and some very small agencies. Only 31 percent in the national, and 16 percent in the Virginia, samples reported using computer-based methods. A surprisingly large number use command discretion—allocations based on the ad hoc judgments of commanders. In the National Sample, it was indicated that about as many as 11 percent reported relying solely on command discretion; in the Virginia Sample, the figure was 53 percent. But an additional 33 percent in the National Sample report using command discretion as a supplement to workload or hazard data; the comparable Virginia figure is 11 percent. This pattern of usage may be taken to suggest reservations among police managers concerning the utility of proportional distribution and computer-based approaches; and reservations, particularly about workload/hazard formulae, were confirmed in the telephone interviews. This pattern of usage may be due in part to the wish to accommodate "political" pressures. It may

be due in part to the fact that present resource allocation techniques do not easily fit the nature of the decision-making process as it is in fact currently practiced in police agencies.

Police resource allocation decision-making is not typically a function confined to the chief executive or any one
management level. The criminal justice literature implies such
a confinement. Rather, such allocation is an interacting process involving responsibility at several layers of the department—chief of police, chief of patrol, captain, lieutenant, and
sergeant, for instance. It is interacting in the sense that the
decisions of one level usually influence the others, and vice
versa. In the National Sample, some 78 percent of the respondents reported that the process was a responsibility at several
levels; in the Virginia Sample the figure was 76 percent. Two
major patterns may be distinguished in the data. The predominant one views the responsibility as extending down at least
to the sergeant level. As one Virginia department reported,
"All levels, from sergeant through chief, are involved in
resource allocation to some degree." Or, as another noted,
"Overall distribution of manpower is ordered by the Chief of
Police through manning levels. However, certain flexibility
exists within each functional area . . . For instance, patrol commanders are allocated a certain number of personnel by the
Captain of Patrol . . . The shift commander and road sergeants
have the flexibility to make adjustments to basic beat assignments in order to direct patrol efforts toward identified problems." Another major pattern is one where the responsibility
is seen as going down only to the captain or bureau command
level. Of those in the National Sample indicating that the
responsibility is layered, some 51 percent report that the process involves all levels down to sergeant; almost 40 percent
indicate that the layers are captain or bureau commander and
above; the balance report lieutenant and above. Of the Virginia departments with layered responsibility 82 percent indicate involvement of all levels to at least the sergeant. Because
these responses were based on assessing formal responsibili-

ties and because the questionnaires were completed by headquarters personnel, the data for first-line supervisor involvement probably have a downward bias.

The nature of the involvement at various levels differs
among locations. Thus, one department can note that, "Line
supervisors recommend; chief makes final decision." Another
can report, "The sergeant in charge makes decisions on a day-
to-day basis. The division commander and chief make decisions usually based on statistics." That the authority of lower-
level line supervisors can be substantial was indicated in the
questionnaire responses. Agencies were asked whether first or
second line supervisors have the authority to make permanent
reallocations of their subordinates without prior approval
from their superiors. The key phrases here are "permanent"
and "without prior approval from their superiors." In the
National Sample, as many as 12 percent responded in the
affirmative; the Virginia figure was 18 percent. But, beyond
this, first-line supervisors in many other departments can
make temporary transfers. This is not surprising, as absence of
such authority would represent a very limited conception of
the first-line supervisor's role. Earlier, it was noted that final
deployments can be unknown to the chief. In another publication, the writer (Farmer, 1980) has mentioned how, for
instance, precinct commanders in the early seventies at each
shift change in New York City used to report deployments on
a dedicated computer system; the data were recognized, however, as unrealistic. Related to this is the matter of phantom
assignments—a tactic, usually for program purposes, of giving
the public or criminally inclined the impression of police
presence which in fact does not exist. Phantom assignments
can be practiced at all levels, e.g., the chief stationing police
officers at opera exits so that powerful citizens will notice a
police presence. But such assignments are more natural at the
operating level.

The allocation process typically is ongoing in a police
agency, involving minor and marginal adjustments. The criminal justice literature does not recognize this characteristic.

The view of the typical department in the literature as being static in its resources allocation between major resource realignments (usually annual) is inaccurate. The continuing or on-going character of the process is clearest when consideration is given not only to "formal" and "permanent" but also to "informal" and "temporary" assignments. One department of 320 officers can report formal reassignments of 2 persons in October, another 3 later in the same month, 2 in November, another 11 later in that month, 2 in February, 6 in March, and so on. Another department with more than 1,200 officers can note, "Too numerous and frequent to list." Major readjustments do occur, and most departments do undertake beat studies. Some 88 percent of the departments in the National, and 71 percent in the Virginia, samples report having undertaken a beat study during the previous five years. (Granted, to look at the other side of the coin, this means that 12 percent in the sample of U.S. cities with populations over 100,000 have not undertaken a beat study in the past five years.) Of those undertaking a beat study, 66 percent in the National Survey and 75 percent in the Virginia Sample report having done so as recently as in 1980 or 1981; some large cities have not done so since 1978 or before.

Nevertheless, some 69 percent of the departments in the National Survey, and 91 percent in the Virginia Sample, report that resources allocation usually involves minor shifts. Further, 74 percent of the respondents noting major shifts indicate that they also make additional minor adjustments. Because many of the adjustments are minor, it can be seen that the rough calculations on which they are based tend to be marginal. Police agencies would not usually describe their calculations as "marginal;" an exception was in the Manpower Allocation Review System (MARS) described in Chapter 7. But the telephone and on-site interviews indicate that the redeployments in a number of departments are based essentially on approximate and ad hoc estimates (frequently qualitative and intuitive) concerning the effects of minor manpower changes on the donor area (or function) and the receiving area or function. When computer-based analyses are undertaken, the calculations (e.g., involving such indicators as response time) are obviously quantitative. In sum, a number of departments undertake what can be described as a loose form of marginal cost-benefit analysis.

Proportional distribution and computer-based techniques are essentially designed to facilitate patrol allocations. Perhaps that is understandable as such a large percentage of police resources are assigned to patrol. But (contrary to the emphasis in the criminal justice literature) resources allocation is not, and should not be, viewed in exclusively geographical terms. Information was solicited in the National and Virginia Samples on all reallocations of resources undertaken during the past year. For a few departments, particularly the large ones, this was a substantial request, and some noted that their reallocations are continuous. Of the reallocations reported, 48 percent were reported as functional, 34 percent as geographic, and 18 percent as both functional and geographic.

Despite these important common features, the operating characteristics of the resources allocation process do vary among U.S. localities. Variations in the use of techniques were mentioned earlier. But, to underscore the variations, let us note the extent to which police resource allocation decisions are made known to the public. In the National Survey, 46 percent of the responding departments indicated that their allocations are public, 41 percent that they are confidential, and 13 percent that they have no clear position. ("No clear position" was described by one agency as "Information is not confidential, but is not intended for public exposure.") No discussion of this feature was found in the criminal justice literature.

IMPLICATIONS

The contemporary police institution is afflicted by a dedication to process that should be displaced by emphasis on purpose. This has been described in the earlier section of this chapter on the general issue of ends and means in policing. It has been illustrated by the account of the case of police resources allocation decision-making, characterized as a triumph of means over ends.

Acceptance of this diagnosis—insufficiency of purpose— lays the path open for the cure. Appropriate emphasis on purpose permits coming to grips with the hydra of bad politics and it allows admission of the good politics that lies at the heart of the new form of police agency. This leads us to a fundamental issue of contemporary policing—the control of political intrusion.

PART II

Policy Formulation

"To let politics become a cesspool, and
then avoid it because it is a cesspool, is
a double crime."
CROSBY

"Purpose without power is weakness;
power without purpose is fatuity."
SADI

CHAPTER 4

Politics and Policing

A fundamental prerequisite for redirecting police institutions toward the new form that is required for effective crime control is frank and creative recognition of the realities of the relationship between policing and politics. Three such realities must be recognized.

First, politics is part of the warp and woof of police decision-making. To varying degrees in different locations and times, political considerations shape much significant decision-making at the lowest, the intermediate, and the highest levels of policing. Even when absent in fact, the political element is potentially present in all police decision-making of consequence.

Second, overreacting to the reality that much political interference with policing has been inimical to the general good, police managers and thinkers—as well as politicians— have been ill-advised in emphasizing that there should be an antiseptic separation of policing and politics. On the contrary, police decision-making can be improved not by denying but by recognizing and manipulating the political element.

Third, a similar recognition must be that, while some instances are harmful, other cases of political interference can be in the public interest. The intrusion of an Adolf Hitler into the German police process in order to extinguish the rights and lives of particular groups is an illustration of a great evil; the intrusion of a local nabob to quash a parking ticket is an example of a small evil. The intrusion of an elected official, on the other hand, in assisting in setting order maintenance goals, in consonance with the intent of both the law and community wishes, may be viewed as consistent with the fundamental principles of democratic government; so may interference in requiring police accountability for crime control performance.

In the new form of police agency, police politics will be seen as essential for effective policing. Police politics in this context will be defined essentially as the setting of order maintenance goals and as the evaluation of community and agency performance in achieving these goals. Denying and resisting all forms of political interference, the contemporary police agency—not yet advanced to the new form—can avoid orientation to purpose and to the longer term. Agencies can be directed toward process, rather than toward purpose. They can develop resources allocation techniques that aim for process goals such as equal workload allocation, for example, and they can remain oblivious to the lack. Agencies can operate essentially on a day-to-day basis, with meaningful longer-term plans being quite foreign and with the objective on Tuesday being little more than to get the city safely to Wednesday. At the same time, politics has been denied but not avoided. The police force, while alleging to be above (or below or beyond) politics, in such circumstances covertly and sometimes unconsciously takes the politics into its own hands. The contemporary police agency operates under a variant of Gresham's law, as bad politics has driven out good (and necessary) police politics. A prerequisite of the new form of police agency is to restore the currency of politics in police policymaking and management.

This chapter illustrates the three realities noted above, with special reference to the case of police resources allocation decision-making. In so doing, it underscores the political character of the new form of police agency. The first contention addressed is that politics permeates police decision-making. This it illustrates by referring to the general considerations about politics and policing advanced in the criminal justice literature, and then by reporting survey data collected on police resources allocation decision-making in U.S. police agencies. The intention here is to do the best that technically can be done to offer significant evidence not inconsistent with the proposition. The second contention is that police decision-making can be improved by recognizing and manipulating the political element. For this purpose, basic conceptual tools of microeconomics are applied as a step in developing a relevant theory of public sector resources allocation decision-making. The third contention is that some cases of political interference can be for the general good. This is done by referencing (again) the relevant criminal justice literature.

PERVASIVE POLITICS

Textbooks on police administration are sparse in their references to the political environment. Thus, the fourth edition of O. W. Wilson's standard textbook on Police Administration can note that "The literature of police administration gives little attention to the problems of the police administrator who encounters 'politics,' as the word is commonly used in the derogatory sense." It then comments that many "police officials . . . believe that a forthright discussion of police and politics is somehow on the forbidden list of thoughts that must remain in verbal form only" (Wilson and McLaren, 1977). Yet there is discussion, albeit of limited utility, of the relationship in the general criminal justice literature.

The interaction between police and politics is multifaceted, complex, and difficult. It is multifaceted in that it covers a wide spectrum of subjects, including—as Knight points out (Knight, 1982)—financing, staffing, policies, laws, administration, operations, standards, and unionism. It is complex in that the impact of the politics–police relationship has a differential impact on various aspects of police activity. James Q. Wilson explains, for example, that the maintenance of order—with the exception of large-scale civil disorders—is hard to bring under administrative (and thus political) control insofar as politics operates through the making of conscious decisions by formal institutions like mayors and city councils (Wilson, 1972). Community choices may have a great effect on police personnel, budget, pay levels, and organization; but they can rarely have more than a limited effect on police operational behavior, especially where the police response is citizen-invoked. The interaction is difficult in that politics is a term enjoying a range of meanings, varying from partisan party politics to bureaucratic self-interest. The model presented later shares the meaning utilized by Cole. He describes criminal justice as justice achieved through bargains, or exchange relationships, arrived at among participants in the process, and influenced by politics, administrative needs, and community environment (Cole, 1980); but other definitions are equally valid. To the extent that these features—facets, complexity, and difficulty—have not been deeply explored, the literature of criminal justice is indeed of limited utility to the police manager confronted with the reality of the political context.

The literature is sufficient to reflect the pervasiveness of the impact of politics on police decision-making in general, however. That police responses to urban crime are determined in important ways by patterns of urban politics was the conclusion of a study of ten large U.S. cities for the period 1948–78 (Beecher et al., 1981). Another study reported that, for policies the authors considered more likely to affect citizens' lives directly (manpower levels and community relations programs), political variables are more important as determinants than environmental influences and crime measures (Morgan et al., 1976). The same importance of political factors is reported in yet another study of police agencies (Abney and

Lauth, 1979). Reporting on a survey of 1979 police chiefs, these authors distinguish three kinds of councilpersons as represented by their relationships with their police agencies. The first they call "informants" (requesting information on police programs); the second they call "mediators" (relaying constituents' complaints about police service delivery and attempting mediation); and the third "procurers." Beyond this, however, it is also recognized in the literature that many police decisions are essentially and inevitably political. O'Brien gives three examples where the police decision is necessarily also political—decisions to use dogs, lethal weapons, and community relations (O'Brien, 1978).

Particular examples abound in the criminal justice literature. Greenblatt notes the politics in the Boston Police Department (Greenblatt, 1980). The importance of political sponsorship in police career advancement was reported by the Massachusetts Legislative Research Council (Mass. Legislative Research Council, 1965). The accounts of the 1966 New York City referendum, which defeated the Civilian Review Board for the Police Department, constitute another example (e.g., Viteritti, 1973). The manipulation of Uniform Crime Reporting data by police in response to pressure from the Nixon Administration is yet another (Seidman and Couzens, 1974). Haller discusses the interrelationship of crime, criminal justice, politics, reform, and ethnicity in Chicago in the early twentieth century (Haller, 1970). The relationship between corruption, politics, and law enforcement, described for Rainfall West (a pseudonym for a city of one million) from 1962 to 1969, is echoed in other jurisdictions (Chambliss, 1971). Jumping to the last century, Miller compares the responses of 19th century New York and London police to the Blue Laws. The New York police differed from the English in not balancing group demands, in not looking beyond the local impact of their practices, and in being subject to the whims of partisan politics (Miller, 1977).

So that the problem is not misrepresented as exclusively American, let us note instances in other countries. Reiner reports what he sees as the growing politicization of the English police over the past fifteen years (Reiner, 1981). He notes the forms. The first is that the police have developed as an overtly political pressure group, lobbying for desired changes; the second is that the character of policing has become more openly political, particularly in relation to public order, to preemptive policing and surveillance, and to strained relationships between police and blacks. Political influences are reported in a variety of other countries. These accounts range from those of the civilized to the barbaric— from Holland (Straver, 1979) and France (Lantier, 1970) to Brazil and its Death Squad (Jakubs, 1977).

The above tells only part of the story. Omitted because it is not central to the present discussion is another form of political influence—politics-by-osmosis. This form is captured in the sociological descriptions of the police occupation and subculture. The police in this branch of inquiry have been described as a "non-ethnic minority" and as a right-wing political group (Keller, 1975), for example. The police tendency to support radical right-wing and conservative politics is described, as another example, as resulting from occupational role and social background (Lipset, 1974)—intolerance associated with lower and lower-middle class origins, job experiences in the ghetto, the police sense of being a "low-status outgroup," and the tendency for liberals and leftists to be concerned with the rights of defendants and police discretion. In a not dissimilar vein, Johnson describes the local public police as a vehicle for working class viewpoints and interests, contrasting in this respect with the rest of the criminal justice system (Johnson, 1976). Writing of Germany, Lautmann characterizes the police as supporting the legitimacy of the existing social system and as being against the lower socioeconomic classes which are seen as dangerous by the elite groups dominating the society (Lautmann, 1971). Hilton advances another view (Hilton, 1972). Because laws are usually out of step with successive generations, police are perceived as supporting the ideals only of the older generation and as having "political attitudes." Ending this digression, it will be noted that it leaves us with a mixed offering—the benefits of insight and all the disadvantages of stereotyping.

Let us add additional information on the pervasiveness of politics, focusing here on police resources allocation decision-making. The survey data presented here were collected from the Police Resources Allocation Decision-Making Survey described in Chapter 1, the study which was also referenced in Chapter 3 (Farmer, 1981).

The survey data support the view that the objectives of the resources allocation process may be directed, variously, toward programmatic, toward bureaucratic, or toward combinations of programmatic and bureaucratic goals. "Programmatic" in this context is used to mean where the process objective is to maximize social welfare by producing optimal program output. Reflecting a traditional view of the public administrator as a public servant, the resource allocator in this programmatic case seeks to achieve the altruistic "public interest" goal—without catering to wishes for modifications in service from individuals or special interests merely because of their political or other clout. "Bureaucratic" here designates where the process objective serves a purpose (usually political) other than the public interest goal—a purpose selected by, or imposed upon, the bureaucrat. The most likely assumption is that the goal of the resource allocator in this bureaucratic case, rather than altruistic, is to seek optimal bureaucratic self-interest directed toward an ultimate objective such as career survival and growth. An alternative assumption under the same heading of "bureaucratic" would be seeking to maximize the welfare of only a segment of society—in return for which the resource allocator would derive some personal benefits, in terms of career, reward, and/or other satisfaction.

Before presenting the survey data on this issue, it would be well to place this matter of process goals in the context of the diversity of views that have been expressed concerning the goals of both private and public enterprise. The goal of the private enterprise firm, for example, traditionally has been held to be that of profit maximization, e.g., Hicks, 1946. But the assumption has been questioned. For instance, Simon (1959) has suggested profit satisficing, and Baumol (1959) has suggested sales (or growth of sales) maximization. Machlup (1967) lists sixteen concerns of the firm. Specification of goals has proven particularly difficult in the case of public enterprise. Formal goals of public enterprise, notes Anne Witte (1980), "While setting a general tone for a public organization, are often seen more as constraints than as things to be maximized." She suggests risk avoidance; Niskanen (1971) proposed budget maximization. The difficulty is further illustrated by the discussion of the possible goal for public managers of minimizing the costs of producing public services. Conrad (1980) reports that hospitals minimize cost in the short, but not the long, run. Getz (1979, 1980) notes that libraries are more inclined to minimize costs than fire departments. Summers (1977, 1979) suggests that cost minimization is of small importance in public school systems, and Phillips (1978) reports that police departments do not effectively cost minimize.

Table 2 shows the percentage of police departments in the National and Virginia samples reporting that, in making resource allocation decisions, consideration is given to the

TABLE 2
Police Departments Reporting the Indicated Inputs in Making
Resource Allocation Decisions, National and Virginia Samples,
1981

	U.S. cities over 100,000		Virginia communities over 5,000	
	N.	Percentage affirmative	N.	Percentage affirmative
Consult interest groups	119	48	45	60
Consult community groups	119	55	45	73

SOURCE: 1981 Police Resources Allocation Survey.

views of interest and community groups. Clearly, the data must be interpreted with caution. First, consulting interest groups is not synonymous with allocating resources in accordance with interest group wishes, and consultation with community groups is consistent with a program (maybe a community-oriented style), as well as a bureaucratic, objective. Second, the data is based on self-reporting by police agencies, with the direction of the bias being dependent on attitude toward the practice reported.

Only a minority of the responding police agencies reported attaching more significance to the views of interest and community groups than to such "programmatic" considerations as relative workloads—6 percent in the National, and 11 percent in the Virginia, samples. The percentages of those reporting affirmatively to eleven selected inputs were (with the National sample data shown first, and the Virginia sample data second, in the respective parentheses) relative workload (98, 87), particular problems (92, 93), response time (74, 82), views of elected officials (60, 69), views of community groups (55, 73), relative peak-hour populations (53, 53), views of different interest groups (48, 60), the particular sensibilities of particular groups (41, 51), preservation of neighborhoods likely to deteriorate without "extra" protection (36, 51), needs of business in deteriorating neighborhoods (27, 52), and income between geographical areas (6, 9). The higher ranking of program considerations, assuming reliability of the self-reported data, may be taken to suggest that there are relatively few completely "bureaucratic" departments among the respondents. Nevertheless, there do seem to be such agencies; Table 3 gives examples from the survey response. Further, the data are, of course, aggregated for each respondent city. These figures do not speak to the issue of the extent to which a number of these departments are (or are not) in this category on a temporary basis—and, in an important sense, it can be argued that all decisions are on a temporary basis. The telephone interviews supported the views that some "normally" programmatic agencies adopt bureaucratic objectives on a tem-

TABLE 3

Examples of Self-Reported b-Goal Police Agencies, Showing the
Factors Reportedly Considered in Allocating Police Resources in
the Designated Cities

	Approximate population served by the agency	Factors considered in allocating resources	Ranking of factors in terms of importance of influence on the decision-making
Dept A	6,500	Views of different interest groups	1st
		Views of community groups	2nd
		Views of elected officials	3rd
Dept B	9,500	Existence of particular problems	1st
		Views of community groups	2nd
		Views of different interest groups	3rd
Dept C	103,000	Existence of particular problems	1st
		Assuage particular sensibilities of particular groups	1st
		Views of different interest groups	1st
		Views of elected officials	1st
		Views of community groups	1st
		Relative workload between geographical areas	2nd
		Relative response time between geographical areas	3rd
Dept D	195,000	Existence of particular problems	1st
		Views of elected officials	2nd
		Views of different interest groups	3rd
Dept E	675,000	Views of elected officials	1st
		Views of different interest groups	2nd
		Existence of particular problems	3rd

Note: To facilitate freedom of response, the names of responding agencies are not
provided.

SOURCE: 1981 Police Resources Allocation Survey.

porary basis and that some departments are predominantly bureaucratic and others predominantly programmatic.

CONTROLLING POLITICAL INTRUSION

Police decision-making, it has been suggested, can be improved not by denying but by recognizing and manipulating the political element. Denial has proven to be a failure on two counts. It has not eliminated those political intrusions that are undesirable, e.g., the influencing of operational practices to provide undue benefits to special interests; on the contrary, such influences are pervasive. Yet those forms of political interference that are desirable—such as goal setting and evaluation by elected officials—have been effectively blocked. The baby has been thrown out with the bath water.

This section suggests an intellectual framework, a basis of understanding, for recognizing and manipulating the political element. Use of this appraoch would move a police institution toward the new form necessary for effective crime control, encouraging not only a realistic but also an open style of decision-making.

The method used in presenting this approach involves the application of some elementary and basic tools of microeconomics to a particular case of police decision-making. That particular case is resources allocation decision-making. Since the publication of Gary Becker's seminal article (Becker, 1968), Economics has demonstrated a potential for contributing significantly to a deeper understanding of law enforcement issues. Perhaps this is not surprising in the case of police resources allocation, as Economics can be defined in Samuelson's words as "the study of how men (sic) and society choose, with or without the use of money, to employ scarce productive resources to produce various commodities over time and distribute them for consumption, now and in the future, among various people and groups in society" (Samuelson,

1951). He could have been defining police resources allocation.

In talking of law enforcement, we are so conditioned to traditional sociological and survey modes of thought that some readers may be distressed by the esoteric character of economic analysis: it may seem so distant from the armpit "real world" of stopping bad guys from hurting people on 42nd Street. Economic analysis proceeds by developing and testing models. In gross terms, the model is developed by specifying a set of assumptions and deducing conclusions about behavior governed by such assumptions. To test the model, deductions can be drawn that predict behavior in selected situations, and these predictions can then be evaluated following empirical measurement. For those unused to economic analysis, the most distressing assumption is that of rationality—that all the actors know how to optimize, know how to get it, and are willing to do what it takes to get it. For those distressed by the abstractions, perhaps it may help to recall that the ultimately more useful and basic discoveries in the physical sciences at first sight could have appeared divorced from human needs and only of academic interest— whether it was Archimedes sitting in his bathtub, Galileo looking through his telescope, or Einstein describing curved space.

The value of such economic analysis, for the present writer, lies in the insights gained. The present analysis provides insights about police resources allocation decision-making, about public sector resources allocation decision-making, and about the control of political intrusion. Concerning police resources allocation, it repairs the deficiency in the current literature by indicating how the political element impacts on the decision-making and by describing the operation of factors shaping the choice of process objective: it provides the conceptualization, the basis, that is needed if more effective techniques for allocating police resources are to be developed. Concerning public sector resources allocation in general, the present model goes far toward suggesting a general theory of public sector resources allocation. There seems to be no persuasive reason to suppose significant dissimilarities between other public sector functions and the police function in terms of resources allocation decision-making. Concerning the control of political intrusion, the model suggests the basic, underlying factors helpful in describing, explaining, and predicting how such decisions are made. It was noted earlier that the model seeks to explain the operation of more fundamental forces, rather than the rationale advanced by the allocators themselves, for the allocation decisions. Such a description is necessary for the development of controls of political influence on order maintenance operations such as police resources allocation decision-making.

The starting point of this analysis is the assumption that the ultimate goal of the resource allocator can be described as programmatic (p-goal), bureaucratic (b-goal), or mixed (p-b goal). These terms are defined in the next few paragraphs. Then it asks three questions. How would the manager, assuming rational behavior, allocate resources if he pursued the p-goal? The b-goal? And the p-b goal? The end point is what is described as a conditional model of police resources allocation decision-making. The designation "conditional" is used to describe the model, because it is demonstrated that conditions determine the choice of goal—the choice of a p-b point. In other words, conditions determine the extent to which resource allocation decisions are politicized. The significance of this conclusion lies in the possibility of controlling or manipulating these conditions.

So let us begin by describing the assumption that the resource allocator's goal can be viewed as programmatic, bureaucratic, or mixed.

The programmatic goal (p-goal) reflects the traditional Public Administration view of the public administrator as the altruistic public servant. Such a p-goal resource allocator is understood to be disinterested in any effects of his programmatic (or bureaucratic) decisions on his own welfare in the bureaucracy. He may or may not derive benefit from his own program in his private capacity as a citizen; but he does not seek any return to himself qua bureaucrat. The goal of the p-goal resource allocator is to achieve the altruistic "public interest." In other words, the goal of such a resource allocator is to maximize social welfare by producing optimal program output.

The bureaucratic goal (b-goal) reflects the pluralist view of the public administrator. It describes the goal of the resource allocator, rather than as altruistic, as seeking optimal bureaucratic self-interest directed toward the self-serving objective of personal career survival and growth. The resource allocator in this case is the bureaucratic equivalent of the "economic man"—the "bureaucratic man." Just as simplifying assumptions are useful in thinking of economic man (e.g., that the returns he wishes to optimize are confined to monetary profits, to increased sales, etc.), so too a simplified view of bureaucratic man is helpful. Rewards unrelated to career furtherance, like the possible selfish pleasure to be derived from working for the public interest, are not included.

The b-goal assumes that the public manager attempts to maximize his own career survival and growth, and it makes the corollary assumption that he allocates his resources (and makes all other managerial decisions) in such a way as to secure maximum effective demand for the career survival and growth of the manager. In very loose terms, it can be said that the b-goal manager makes decisions (including allocation decisions) in order to "satisfy" the self-interest of his superior and the self-interest of the interest groups and individuals impacting upon his superior. (The manager's superior is understood as the person or people with effective control over the manager's career survival and growth, e.g., a partisan party clique, a committee, or a mayor.) The manager maximizes this return to the bureaucracy (this effective demand)—in a fashion similar to maximizing the profit accruing to the entrepreneur in the case of the private firm. This return or effective demand we will term "bureaucratic welfare," and this notion will be further discussed three paragraphs below.

The b-goal perspective noted above is founded on the literature of Management, Public Administration, and Political Science, particularly work undertaken since World War II. The notions of bureaucratic self-interest have been developed by writers like Downs and Tullock, and, as Downs explains (Downs, 1967), "this theory follows the tradition of economic thought from Adam Smith forward, and is consistent with recent contributions to political science made by such writers as Simmel, Truman, Schattschneider, Buchanan, Tullock, Rieker, and Simon." The notion of administrators as persons dealing with sets of interest groups now dominates Public Administration literature (e.g., Truman, 1951, Lowi, 1969; Sharkansky, 1975). Since Truman (1951), the pluralists have been a major force in Political Science and Public Administration.

The b-goal formulation of the nature of the bureaucrat's self-interest exhibits both similarities and differences compared with views advanced by a number of others. The b-goal refers only to career survival and growth. Downs was more general in his specification of the general motives of officials (Downs, 1967), including also power, prestige, and convenience. Breton offered the elegantly simple but perhaps more questionable view that officials wish to maximize power (Breton, 1974)—and the view was questioned by Jo Grimmond in 1978 (Grimmond, 1978). Niskanen follows Downs in suggesting "the several variables that may enter the bureaucrat's motives"—"salary, perquisites of office, public reputation, power, patronage, output of the bureau, ease of making changes, and ease of managing the bureau." He then unifies this by pointing out that "[a]ll except the last two are a positive function of the total budget of the bureau during the bureaucrat's tenure" (Niskanen, 1971). Perhaps this perspective is understandable from one who was once Assistant Director of the Office of Management and Budget.

The return to the bureaucracy in the b-goal, as was noted, is here termed "bureaucratic welfare." Other terms such as "leverage" or "clout" are feasible, although some may argue that the latter have the disadvantage of more established connotations not shared by the newer term "bureaucratic welfare."

Five characteristics of such bureaucratic welfare are assumed. First, both positive and negative bureaucratic welfare are assumed to exist. Positive bureaucratic welfare would be leverage helpful for the manager's purpose of career survival and growth, e.g., support from a powerful community group for his continued employment. Negative bureaucratic welfare would be leverage intended to frustrate the manager's purpose, e.g., to get the manager fired. Second, a holder of bureaucratic welfare may use his supply of such welfare either for positive or negative objectives. Positive bureaucratic welfare not used as such, for example, can be transformed at will and utilized as negative bureaucratic welfare. Third, it is assumed that each person at any one time has a fixed amount of bureaucratic welfare at his disposal. A plutocrat usually has more bureaucratic welfare (or leverage or clout), for example, than a pauper. Like assets or income, this fixed amount may vary over time—just as it does between people. The fourth characteristic is that bureaucratic welfare is a depletable item. Because of limitations such as time, for instance, energies (or bureaucratic welfare) spent in achieving a particular objective (such as securing one official's survival) are assumed to diminish the supply of bureaucratic welfare available for other objectives. A person may use bureaucratic welfare (or leverage) in lobbying simultaneously for officials X and Y, just as the consumer can spend money simultaneously on bacon and eggs. But the stock of bureaucratic welfare spent for official Y is assumed—reasonably—to be additional to that expended for official X. The fifth is that the propensity to spend bureaucratic welfare may vary between persons.

The mixed (p-b goal) treats both the programmatic and the bureaucratic assumptions as polar extremes, and it provides a bridge between the two limiting cases. Under the programmatic assumption, the resource allocator has the altruistic objective of pursuing the public interest—of optimizing social welfare. Under the bureaucratic assumption, the resource allocator has the goal of seeking his own self-interest—of optimizing his own bureaucratic welfare. The mixed goal describes the resource allocator as choosing one from among the variety of self-interest/altruistic-interest points that range from one pole to the other. It continues to assume, as in the p- and b-goals, that the resource allocator is a benefit-maximizer. In this case, he is a person who wishes to maximize benefits to himself and/or to others.

The p-b goal, then, conceptualizes the resource allocator's goal-seeking as constituting a choice of one from a range of self-interest/altruistic-interest points. Let the range be viewed, for expository purposes, as a line showing the relative intensities of the two goals for the resource allocator. At the end of the line (p), the sole goal is altruistic, maximizing social welfare. At the other end (b), the sole goal is selfish, maximizing bureaucratic welfare. At intermediate points, the resource allocator has two goals. As he moves farther from p, the bureaucratic welfare goal is pursued to increasing extents— from zero at p, through degrees of sub-maximum to a maximum at b. In this conceptualization, the intensity of altruistic goal-seeking is a reciprocal of self-interest goal-seeking; and vice versa. A limitation of such a conceptualization is that no provision is made for the goal-seeker to have no goal-seeking; such a provision concerning goals is not possible here because it is assumed that the resource allocator wishes to maximize benefits to himself and/or to others. Just as the entrepreneur in economic analysis is assumed to be goal-seeking (e.g., profit maximizing, profit satisficing, or sales maximizing), so too the resource allocator in the mixed position is assumed to have a goal or goals.

How would the manager, assuming rational behavior, allocate resources in pursuing the programmatic goal (p-goal)? Four features are clear, and are noted in the next seven paragraphs. First, the answer is straightforward in principle. The public agency will seek to maximize social welfare by producing as close as possible to optimal output—the output where net social benefit (social benefit minus social cost) is largest. With no budget constraint, the agency will allocate resources to a particular need (or area) to the point where the marginal social benefit equals—as Stigler (1970) and others have pointed out—marginal social cost. With a budget constraint, resources will be allocated (where MB = marginal benefit and MC = marginal cost) so that:

$$\frac{MB_a}{MC_a} = \frac{MB_b}{MC_b} = \cdot \cdot \cdot \cdot \cdot = \frac{MB_n}{MC_n}$$

The observation has been made that police and other agencies may well not be concerned with minimizing agency operating costs (e.g., Heinecke, 1978; Phillips, 1978). If this observation is accepted, a decision model (in the case where there is a budget constraint and where the optimal order level has not been reached) can be specified in purely "programmatic" terms. Marginal benefit (i.e., marginal contribution to reduction of social cost) would be the only criterion. Cost would enter only in such terms as opportunity cost. The opportunity cost in terms of social benefit for an output delivered at (or factor employed at) a particular geographical point should not be greater than for its delivery (or employment) at any other point. In the unconstrained budget case, the p-model resource allocator inevitably would be concerned with police costs. Wastage of police resources would constitute a social cost, an entity which the p-goal resource allocator is concerned to minimize.

Second, the concept of social welfare (and the derivative notions in this case of benefit and costs) is far from straightforward. Chapter 5 will describe how it is useful to recognize that order production cannot, and should not, be viewed as an end in itself. Further, it is not easy for the practitioner to operationalize the notion of optimal socio-economic activity. Some agencies, somewhat in the spirit of Bergson–Samuelson, do seek community input for their program activities; 55 percent in the National Sample and 73 percent in the Virginia Sample reported consulting community views on resources allocation decisions, for example. This may involve some indirect consideration of social welfare. Most police agencies do not define their goals in terms of society's welfare, however. Many continue to view their activities in terms of means, rather than ends—and perhaps this is encouraged by the difficulty of operationalizing such notions as social welfare.

Third, elementary economic concepts can be utilized to flesh out the p-goal. This can be demonstrated by considering the production function in the law enforcement case and the relevance of marginal revenue productivity in this situation. A law enforcement production function specifies the maximum obtainable output available from a set of inputs; a value here is that it makes it necessary to specify the factors (the inputs) of police production. The traditional textbook categorization of law enforcement inputs into capital and labor is of limited utility. A similar need to reformulate inputs has been identified elsewhere in the public sector—for example, by Conrad (1980) in relation to hospitals, and by Getz (1980) in relation to libraries. Specification of inputs does have a certain arbitrary character. At a primary or unaggregated level, the factors of police production would certainly include labor and quasi-free labor. Less aggregated levels of inputs may be identified, e.g., labor in this case refers to both sworn and civilian personnel.

The second factor of police production is quasi-free labor, a notion described as follows. Police agencies routinely receive quasi-free inputs. Other public agencies, groups, and individuals, for example, often wish to provide input to the police agency. Thus, firefighters may be made available to a police agency in searching for a missing child; citizens may volunteer to patrol the streets in an effort to help the police. Certainly quasi-free inputs are not peculiar to policing. Firefighting and hospitals are examples of areas where volunteerism is strong. Quasi-free is a better description than, simply, free inputs. They are not free goods. First, the supply of such inputs—unlike free goods—is not virtually unlimited. From the viewpoint of hospital economics, volunteers should be regarded differently from fresh air. Second, the supply of quasi-free inputs can usually be affected by agency expenditure. Public relations activity, for example, can be expected to increase the supply of police volunteers—the supply of police informants for a police agency, as well as the supply of tax informants for income tax agencies. Third, the public agency—as was noted above—is involved in costs if it wishes to utilize quasi-free inputs. When one person helps a police officer, there will not usually be additional cost. But when ten thousand help, expenditures may be necessary. Private entrepreneurs in the rational model cannot expect to receive any inputs free; police and other public agencies routinely receive quasi-free labor. It is not paid labor; nor is it free, since the public agency, for instance, must expect to invest in planning and action programs if it wishes to utilize such quasi-free inputs. Thus, the production function for policing can be written as:

$$y = f(L,Q)$$

where y = output, L = labor, and Q = quasi-free labor. The demand for police labor to be assigned to a particular area (or function) is a jointly interdependent derived demand, and the production function specifies the nature of this interdependence. The marginal benefits in any area will be conditioned by the production function of that area. The character of this function will be significant for labor allocation decisions, clearly.

Proceeding beyond this, let us note that the matter of the demand for an input is a well-trodden subject in the economic theory of the firm. In simple terms, a firm's demand curve for a factor such as labor is given by the input factor's marginal revenue product—the marginal physical product of labor $\times$ the marginal revenue accruing from the quantity added; and, speaking generally, the competitive firm will be at equilibrium where the marginal revenue product equals the price of the input. On this basis, it would be expected that the police agency would seek to allocate labor resources so that the marginal revenue product of police labor (marginal physical product × contribution of that marginal product to order maintenance) equals the marginal revenue product of quasi-free labor—each marginal revenue product being divided by its respective cost. The relative susceptibility of labor and quasi-free labor to adjustment by the police agency is a matter for empirical research. But it is unlikely that they are equal. A reasonable assumption is that in the shorter run a police agency is able to adjust only its allocation of labor. It would also be expected, with other things being equal, that the police agency would allocate labor resources so that the marginal revenue product of police labor at any point would equal the marginal revenue product of the labor assigned to any other geographical point. It will be noted that the marginal benefits calculation (on the basis of the marginal revenue product) is the product of the "marginal order maintenance service output of labor" and the "potential of that service to contribute to the required order level."

Fourth, this formulation of the p-goal provides a framework for examining resource allocation techniques. On the basis indicated above, for example, workload/hazard formulae and current computer models involve a narrower definition of benefits than seems desirable. It was indicated that the marginal benefit calculation on these lines would be the product of the marginal order maintenance service output and the marginal potential for impact on order levels. This concept is present in neither workload/hazard formulae nor in current models based on such criteria as response time. Faced with two areas equal in all respects except that the probability of success (e.g., in reducing crime) is much higher in one than in the other, workload/hazard formulae would invite the manager to allocate equal resources in each area. It should be noted that the potential that is critical in this case is the marginal, not the average or initial, probability. The same is true of computer models that seek to equalize response times or similar characteristics; they do not (although they could) consider the varying potential of response time to impact different situations in different areas. Possibly this accounts for the continuing reliance (discussed earlier) of a surprising number of departments on command discretion as a means of resource allocation.

How would the rational manager allocate resources in pursuit of the bureaucratic goal (b-goal)? This alternative assumes that the resource allocator, aiming for an ultimate objective such as career survival and growth, seeks to obtain maximum net bureaucratic welfare—leverage from individuals and groups, mainly outside the agency, effective for the ultimate purpose.

Orthodox microeconomic analysis, despite absence of monetary numeraire, can be used to explain the mechanics of the b-goal. There is no "difficulty" in constucting a demand curve showing the relationship between the quantity of order maintenance service demanded and the price of various levels of service in terms of bureaucratic welfare (or leverage) required per unit of such order maintenance service. This curve could be constructed for an individual, for individuals in a particular area, or for all individuals in the jurisdiction. In the traditional way, quantity would be shown along one axis (the abscissa) and price along the other (the ordinate). The demand curve for all except free-riders can be expected to slope downward and to the right. Traditional indifference curve analysis could be applied in developing such demand schedules.

Similarly, there is no difficulty in drawing a supply curve, indicating the relationship between the amount of order maintenance service provided by the police agency and the amount of bureaucratic welfare per unit of order maintenance received as a consequence by the supplying agency. Such a supply curve, of course, could be expected to slope upwards and to the right. Two further characteristics of such a supply curve may be noticed. First, the shape will vary between jurisdictions. For instance, in jurisdictions where the police are relatively more immune from political influence, the supply curve will differ from that for jurisdictions more open to political influence. Second, the shape will vary over time. Where a government is elected on a four-year fixed-term basis, for instance, the supply curve in the year after the election could be expected to shift from its position in the fourth year. Equilibrium would be at the point, naturally, where the demand and supply curves intersect.

The traditional theory of the firm can be used to describe the behavior of the police agency. Positive leverage can supply the basis for drawing the revenue curves. Negative leverage would permit drawing the cost curves. The latter, of course, refers not only to the direct negative effect on people (e.g., giving a speeder a ticket) but also to the opportunity cost of the service—the cost in terms of negative leverage from B resulting from allocating positive service instead to A. The police agency can be expected to produce that output that allows it to equate marginal revenue in terms of positive bureaucratic welfare and marginal cost expressed in terms of negative bureaucratic welfare.

Let us be more precise. With no budget constraint, police manpower in the b-goal case will be allocated to the level where the marginal benefit (in terms of positive bureaucratic welfare) that is declining is equal to the price (in terms of negative bureaucratic welfare) of that factor. With a budget constraint, police order maintenance resources will be allocated so that the marginal utility to the resources allocator (in terms of bureaucratic welfare) of resources assigned to one usage is equal to the marginal utilities of resources assigned to all other usages.

These conclusions can be extended to include consideration of spatial factors as is indicated in the following comments on demand and supply. (It may be noted that neoclassical economic analysis largely excludes consideration of the effects of spatial relationships.) In the b-goal situation described here, resources are viewed as being supplied and demanded with respect to a number of geographic points. The demand for delivery at any point is a composite of individual demands. For instance, how many people exercise effective

demand for order maintenance at the Statue of Liberty—or at
any private house? It is possible that such demand could be
made by many who neither live at, nor visit, those places. It
is also possible that a particular individual may exercise
demand for order maintenance to be delivered at more than
one point, e.g., at the living, working, playing, and other
points. Demand at any point is the aggregate of the demands
with respect to that point. Viewing resources as being
demanded and supplied in respect to a succession of geographical points, the earlier conclusion can be extended. With
no budget constraints, police manpower will be allocated at
each geographic point to the level where the marginal benefit
(in terms of positive bureaucratic welfare) that is declining is
equal to the price (in terms of negative bureaucratic welfare)
of that factor.

Police agencies are structured so that they have some
monopoly powers in relation to the supply of order maintenance. The standard textbook diagram of the monopoly firm
could be used to depict the situation. Certainly there are some
substitutes, e.g., private police, some overlapping public
police coverage. But to the extent that police agencies have
such monopoly power, b-goal agencies may be expected in
some cases to restrict the supply of order maintenance service
in order to increase the return of net bureaucratic welfare. In
this, the b-goal agency would act in the same way as the
monopoly firm—setting price where marginal revenue inter-
sects with marginal cost and obtaining a monopoly profit.
Thus, b-goal police agencies may experience "excess" labor
and other resources—resources which are used by resource
allocators on activities that may be "wasteful" from the order
maintenance viewpoint. Examples of such "excess" labor uses
may be using police for "non-police" purposes such as for typing activities.

How would the rational manager allocate resources in the
mixed situation (p-b goal)? The mixed goal provides a bridge
between the two limiting cases of the p-goal and the b-goal.
The p-b goal assumes that the resource allocator chooses from

among the variety of altruistic-interest/self-interest positions that range between the two limiting cases, it will be recalled.

Four points are of particular significance in this range of options. The range can be conceptualized (it was noted earlier) as the line p-b, showing a steadily increasing proportion of available resources that the resource allocator wishes to invest in the altruistic-interest $vs.$ self-interest goals. The first point is at one end of the line (p). Here the sole goal would be to maximize social welfare, and this is the point explored in the earlier discussion of the p-goal. The second point is at the other end of the line (b), where the goal would be to maximize net bureaucratic welfare. This point was examined in the earlier analysis of the b-goal. As the resource allocator moves from b to p, the proportion of resources allocated to the p-goal will increase. At some point, the resource allocator will have invested sufficient resources for the altruistic-interest purpose where he judges that the social welfare produced is sufficient. This point may lie between b and p; on the other hand, it may be unreachable with current resources and lie beyond p. This, then, is the third point—the sufficiency point for the altruistic-interest purpose (S_p). Conversely, as the resource allocator moves from p toward b, the proportion of resources allocated to the b-goal objective will increase. At some point, the manager will have invested sufficient resources to achieve the ultimate goal of career survival and growth. This is the fourth point—the sufficiency point for the self-interest purpose (S_b). Again, this point may lie between b and p. Alternatively, it may be unattainable with current resources and lie beyond b.

Points S_p and S_b have different characteristics. Assuming that resource allocators are benefit maximizers (aiming to maximize benefits to themselves and/or to others), two major differences between these positions can be noted. First, if S_b (the sufficiency point for bureaucratic welfare) involves more resources than are available, the b-goal objective is not viable. In that case, a benefit maximizer would select either point p or S_p if $S_p < p$, as any other alternative would fail to maximize benefits. By contrast, even if S_p (the sufficiency point for p-goal purposes) involves more resources than are available, investment in the p-goal objective remains a viable option. Second, if S_p is between points p and b, a rational benefit maximizer would allocate the excess resources (those between points S_b and p) for the p-goal purpose. On the other hand, if S_p is between points b and p, a benefit maximizer would allocate excess resources (those between S_p and b) for b-goal purposes only if the amount thus available for the latter at least equalled S_b. Because of its critical character, the current analysis focuses on the determinants of S_b—the sufficiency point for b-goal purposes.

The position of S_b would depend on the interaction of demand and supply conditions. Each of these conditions is considered in turn below. But two points may be noted here. First, understanding of these conditions is policy-relevant for those with objectives such as reducing (or augmenting) the b-goal emphasis in police resources allocation. Second, an alternative formulation would be to describe S_b in terms of a range of sufficiency. Below one end of the range of sufficiency, the proportion of resources invested for b-goal purposes would be insufficient; beyond the other end of the range, the proportion invested would be excessive. Within the range, the resource allocator could expect greater assurance of the superior's support as more resources are invested for b-goal purposes.

A key determinant of the S_b position is the demand from the resource allocator's superior for bureaucratic welfare. This superior was described earlier as the person(s) able to control the resource allocator's survival and growth, e.g., a mayor, a commission, or a party clique. The demand by the rational resource allocator for bureaucratic welfare is partly a derived demand, depending on the goals and circumstances of the resource allocator's superior. If the superior does not have his own career survival and growth (or an equivalent goal) as his ultimate objective, the superior would have no demand for bureaucratic welfare from the resource allocator. In this case, the price of the resource allocator's career survival and growth in terms of bureaucratic welfare would be infinitely high, because bureaucratic welfare would then be valueless as a medium for purchasing career survival and growth. If the superior does have career survival and growth (or an equivalent) as an ultimate objective and if this objective can be realized by obtaining bureaucratic welfare, the superior's demand will be a partial determinant of the resource allocator's demand; other factors will include the resource allocator's preferences on this issue. In the same way, the superior's demand is a derived demand—a demand derived from that of the person(s) able to control the superior's survival and growth (or equivalent ultimate objective).

The superior's demand for bureaucratic welfare from the resource allocator at a point in time can be expressed in such terms as:

$$D_S = f(R_S, B_S^+, B_S^-, S_S, C_S, E_S, T_S, F_S)$$

where D_S = Quantity demand by the superior from the resource allocator.

R_s = Gross quantity of net bureaucratic welfare required by the superior for career survival and growth (e.g., for re-election) or for an equivalent goal.

B_S^+ = Quantity of positive bureaucratic welfare accumulated by the superior.

B_S^- = Quantity of negative bureaucratic welfare accumulated by the superior. Such negative bureaucratic welfare is at least of two major types. The first is that which derives from responsibility for the mere existence of a particular program (e.g., some who dislike authority may express B^- for any police administrator; some who are pacifists may express B^- for any military commander). The second is that resulting from the manner in which the program is carried out.

S_S = Quantity of net bureaucratic welfare available from substitute sources. A mayor, for example, may obtain bureaucratic welfare not only from the police chief but also from other program managers (e.g., fire chief, sanitation manager)—not only from one police resource allocator, but from the other police allocators.

C_S = Quantity of bureaucratic welfare required from the resource allocator in order to obtain other bureaucratic welfare from complementary sources.

E_S = Expectations of the superior concerning future characteristics of the above factors.

T_S = Tastes and preferences of the superior.

F_S = All other relevant factors influencing D_S.

Time is a significant dimension for this demand function. The quantity of net bureaucratic welfare to be used for career survival and growth (R_S) is required by the superior (or any other with a b-goal objective) at such times as decisions are made about the superior's career survival and growth. For some, the decisions are made periodically—either at regular intervals (e.g., for a governor seeking re-election every four years) or irregularly (e.g., for a prime minister without a fixed term of office). For others, decisions are made on a month-by-month, or virtually continuous, basis. Accumulations of positive bureaucratic welfare (B^+) and negative bureaucratic welfare (B^-), as ordinary observation seems to suggest, may be expected to deteriorate over time. The speed of such deterioration and the shape of the deterioration curve are matters for empirical study, and it is possible that the characteristics of the deteriorations may be influenced by a number of variables including the sizes and social characteristics of locations. The other variables (S_S, C_S, E_S), while perhaps less likely to vary than the three noted above, may also show changes over time.

The notion of "decision days" may be helpful in this connection. "Decision days" are defined as those times when decisions are made concerning an individual's career survival and growth. For an elected politician, for example, decision days would include election day and a period before that day (e.g., six weeks or eighteen months, depending on the particular situation) when the superior's superior is forming his opinion. The extent to which a superior would demand bureaucratic welfare on a non-decision day would depend in part on the rate at which B^+ and B^- deteriorate—a technical characteristic of bureaucratic welfare. Let the technical characteristics of units of bureaucratic welfare be such that they deteriorate so that at the end of period t the value of a unit is zero. Then the demand for bureaucratic welfare from the superior would be zero at or before the date of t minus the beginning of the set of decision days—so long as the dates were later than the end of the previous set of decision days. In this case, the intervening period between the "date" and the preceding set of decision days would be one where the superior who is a benefit maximizer would have no b-goal demand.

It may well be that in a particular location the rate of accumulation of B^+ in non-decision days is large enough in relation to need (R_s) and the rate of deterioration of B_s^+ is so protracted that a larger demand from the superior for bureaucratic welfare will not be experienced in the decision-days period as compared with the non-decision days period. Where these two conditions do not hold, there will be (other things being equal) an increase in the superior's demand for bureaucratic welfare during the decision-day period.

Choice between substitute and police sources of B^+ would be on the same basis as selecting optimal input mixes for the firm. In the long run, the combination of inputs will be chosen for which the marginal product of each input (valued in terms of B^+) is equal to the input's prices (valued in terms of B^-). Thus, substitutes will be chosen at least as long as they are available on better terms.

The demand function in the equation, it should be stressed, relates only to demand at a point in time. It is clear that D_s can be viewed, subject to the comments offered above, as discounted in terms of the time from the relevant "decision-days."

The supply conditions for bureaucratic welfare from a resource allocator can be described in general terms such as the following:

$$S_{B+} = f(K_R, I_R, E_R, U_B, N_R, P_R, O)$$

where S_{B+} = Supply of net bureaucratic welfare provided by the resource allocator to his superior

K_R = Supply of bureaucratic welfare available to the resource allocator in the jurisdiction (or area) served by that allocator

I_R = Availability of input resources to the resource allocator for trading for K so that he can supply net positive bureaucratic welfare to the superior

E_R = Decisions by the resource allocator concerning order maintenance effectiveness and efficiency, a substitute source of bureaucratic welfare

U_B = Public understanding of I and E, another substitute source of bureaucratic welfare

N_R = Need of resource allocator to supply bureaucratic welfare in terms of his career survival and growth and his sufficiency point

P_R = Propensity of resource allocator to supply bureaucratic welfare to his superior, a factor dependent on the resource allocator's tastes and preferences

O = All other factors affecting the supply of B by the resource allocator.

The trading relationship between the resource allocator and the public holding bureaucratic welfare was noted earlier in the comments on the allocation of police manpower resources in the b-goal situation. Inclusion of K_R here reflects this in a simplified form. The term K_R is intended to be understood as the amount of bureaucratic welfare available to the police agency after alternative trading (e.g., from other public or private agencies) has been completed.

The availability of resources (I_R) for use by the resource allocator in "supplying" bureaucratic welfare would be the net quantity of resources (e.g., police officers) available to the resource allocator for trading with the public holding bureaucratic welfare. The gross figure would be the number of inputs capable of producing order maintenance service (police officers) that could be utilized in the exchange process. The net quantity would be this same number discounted by the programmatic demand on the services of these units. Programmatic demand in this case would consist of the volume of disorder requiring police attention by the same input units.

Changes in order maintenance effectiveness and efficiency (E_R) and changes in public understanding (U_B) do constitute sources of positive bureaucratic welfare, altering the need to use resource allocation for producing the required welfare. Relative to substitute factors, resource allocation is usually more susceptible to large-scale readjustment in the shorter run. Most police agencies employ a substantial proportion of their manpower on preventive patrol, an activity where time is uncommitted and where performance measures have proved difficult to develop. The barriers to reallocation are relatively smaller in an organization which has as its mission to be a flexible response force to crises; for example, many improvement efforts in policing have been directed at increasing response capability, e.g., use of vehicles, more sophisticated communications equipment. To the extent that such conditions do not exist in some locations at some times, this greater susceptibility to readjustment in the shorter run will not be present. Some changes in E_R and U_B may be effected in the shorter run, e.g., solving a well-publicized homicide, or planting a favorable news story. But such changes are more likely to require a longer time period. For example, a change in E_R may require better cooperation with segments of the public or with other institutions of government.

The propensity of the resource allocator to supply his superior with bureacratic welfare was discussed earlier in this subsection. This propensity was noted to be a function of the allocator's tastes and preferences (P_R). It must also be a factor of his situation in terms of his career survival and growth and of his sufficiency point for bureaucratic welfare (N_R).

The proportion of resources in the p-b goal situation that are allocated to b-goal purposes can be expected to depend on two barter interactions. One is the exchange between the resource allocator and the "public;" the former holds order maintenance service units and the latter possesses bureaucratic welfare. Another is the exchange between the resource allocator and the superior; the former provides the bureaucratic welfare purchased from the "public(s)" and the latter holds the resource allocator's career survival and growth. Expressing the tendency to b-goal allocation solely in terms of the superior's demand schedule and the resource allocator's supply schedule thus requires the simplifying assumption that other things remain equal. One item understood as remaining constant is the supply schedule of each of the other resource allocators in the "market" with the same superior. Another item is the exchange process between the resource allocator and the "public(s)."

Subject to such simplifying assumptions, the resources in the p-b situation that can be expected to be assigned to b-goal purposes will be a function of such demand and supply factors as those noted in the previous equations. The situation can be summarized as follows:

$$MA_{\to b} = f(D_S, S_R)^t$$

Where $MA_{\to b}$ = Extent to which allocations are made on a b-goal basis

D_S = Superior's demand schedule

S_R = Resource allocator's supply schedule

t = Discounted for time before decision-day.

The superscript t is shown in this equation to signify the influence of time. Comments were offered in the discussion on the superior's demand schedule concerning the relevance of time before the appropriate "decision-days." It may be anticipated that a longer time interval would correlate with a larger discount in demand. Time could also be relevant for the supply schedule in a circumstance such as where the resource allocator is appointed for a renewable fixed term. However, in the usual situation where the resource allocator's career survival and growth is "at the pleasure" of the superior, the decision day is in effect continuous and then time would not be relevant in shaping the supply schedule.

IMPLICATIONS

This analysis provides heuristic beginning points in deepening understanding of resources allocation decision-making. The uses are clear. Comment has been made in discussing the p-goal concerning the inadequacies of proportional distribution and current computer-based techniques. Even more obviously, current resources allocation approaches do not meet needs under the b-goal or p-b goal. These inadequacies should be, and are, reflected in the relatively low usage (described in Chapter 3) of workload/hazard and computer-based models for resource allocation purposes. Beyond this, however, the analysis offers insights on the forces underlying political intrusion in police decision-making and on how these forces may be manipulated. The conditional model presents policy makers and managers with the prospect that they need not be merely the victims of political influence; such influences can be manipulated and regulated.

At least three classes of political intrusion in police decision-making can be distinguished. The first are those that are improper—clearly harmful to the public good. The politician who fixes the result of an investigation in favor of his own interests; the influential citizen who secures an allocation of resources at the expense of the less influential; the business man who receives unduly favorable police attention . . . such cases are clear in principle, although harder to identify in the maelstrom of practice. The second are those political intrusions that are questionable, and here the list is more difficult to compile. Situations in which interventions have been described as questionable include those involving promotions and assignments, planned police response in emergency situations, police tactics in coping with demonstrations and riots, and attempts to give control of the police to community groups (Boyle, 1979). To the extent that it permits manipulation of the forces underlying such politicization, the conditional model provides a basis for working for greater freedom from such influences.

Concern at preventing these two types of intrusion has led to blockage of the third category—where political intrusion is desirable. What sort of intrusion would fall into this latter category? The answer, it is suggested, lies in policy formulation and program accountability. More specifically, detailed goal setting and effective program evaluation are the necessary political intrusions. The goal setting must be detailed in that it would identify a set of priorities, longer and shorter term, for order enhancement in various communities and streets of the city. The order enhancement activities must then be evaluated in terms of the goals established. Neither of these two activities can be achieved effectively without the involvement of elected officials, working in partnership with the police "professionals."

Turned inward, the contemporary police institution is suffering from deep bureaucratic malaise that can be broken only by opening the lines to an effective working relationship between the political and the programmatic—between the politician and the administrator. Dedicated too much to process and to the professional model, it places undue reliance on routines that lack clear and meaningful purpose. The new form of institution, being purpose-oriented and accountable, requires political involvement. It will be an open institution to the same extent that the contemporary police agency is closed. As a beginning, communities can address the three realities of police–political relations noted in this chapter. They must accept that politics permeates policing; that police decision-making can be improved not by denying but by recognizing and manipulating the political element; and that, while some are bad, certain political intrusions are necessary and desirable for fully effective performance.

CHAPTER 5

Purpose and Policing

First on the agenda of policy issues for a community seriously concerned with effective crime control and with the quality of life should be public and realistic consideration, and continuing *open* consideration, of the mission and purposes of the police agency. Without appropriate definition of agency goals and purposes, police resources cannot be allocated with maximum effect: without optimal allocations, crime control and other results can only be disappointing. That "police departments do whatever police departments do" is a sociological reality in many communities, as agencies continue to be dominated by considerations of process and tradition. In such agencies, the principal determinant of today's allocation of resources (to choose this major function as an example) is yesterday's allocation. The professional police agenda, centering on a striving for results, will soon feel the effects of goal-orientation. The new form of police agency, with its goals and purposes developed in consultation with the community, will be in an even stronger position to deliver.

This chapter presents a socio-economic view of the purpose of policing. Considered in conjunction with the multi-

plicity of descriptions already in the literature, this conceptualization appears particularly helpful in a world which
appreciates the wide discretion thrust upon the police manager. That police agencies enjoy inevitable and considerable
discretion in their work has been well established; for example, see Fisk's analysis of the decision to arrest or not to arrest
(Fisk, 1973). Within limits, the police officer can determine
which laws to enforce and how to do so: the traffic offender is
often acutely aware of this. Within much wider limits, the
police manager can prioritize and shape law enforcement
practice—through crack-downs, through directions to deem-
phasize or ignore, and through resource allocation decisions.
New York has laws prohibiting art theft and organized crime,
for example; equally as important as the legislators' decision
to pass the relevant laws is the Police Commissioner's discretion to determine the sizes of the Art Theft Squad and the
Organized Crime Bureau. This chapter comments on the
sociological literature related to the mission of the police. It
then offers a conceptualization of the police mission that has
special relevance to the fact of managerial discretion and to
the operation of the new form of police agency.

RANGE OF VIEWS

The literature on the police function offers a variety of
formulations and emphases in describing the police mission.
From this variety, described in the following paragraphs,
three major conclusions may be drawn. First, it seems well-
recognized in the criminal justice literature that it is inappropriate to specify police purpose in terms only of crime control
or law enforcement (e.g., see Wilson, 1975; Goldstein, 1977;
Manning, 1978). Second, while supplementary or alternative
formulations can offer additional insight, it is not inappropriate to describe the purpose of policing in such terms as
"order maintenance." The police in this way are conceived as
peacekeepers and not as law enforcers, with the law being one

of several tools used by the police for the purpose of order maintenance (e.g., see Rumbaut *et al.*, 1979). Social service can be seen as another tool, used for the end of order maintenance. Third, the explanation of the police mission as order maintenance—while clearly useful in terms of deepening understanding—stops short of being completely satisfactory. The concept of "order" is difficult to define; so is the term "disorder." The barking dog in one neighborhood or to one person may constitute disorder and therefore require police action. In a noisier and more disorderly neighborhood or to another person, the same volume of barking may not be considered disorderly or therefore to require police action. The explanation is unsatisfactory, in effect, because we need to know how much order a police agency should provide—the subject of the second part of this chapter.

It is recognized, as a beginning, that the police role must be forged within the environmental context of the agency, and this environment will influence the shaping of the role. Among the environmental factors described in the literature as especially significant for role formulation are the work situation, the law, the character of the community, and the police subculture. The work situation has been described, for example, in such terms as those of ambiguity, changing mores, and violence. The ambiguity has been indicated by noting that the police are required to satisfy the divergent demands of different social classes, being expected to enforce the law and not to enforce the law at the same time (Wilson, 1963). The police, as Wilson adds, cannot take formal rules too seriously because they must maintain good relations with informants and they must obtain information with rough and sometimes illegal methods. Changing mores, the breakdown in absolute definitions of morality, has placed a strain on all social control agents, especially the police (Lawson, 1981).

The violence common in the urban environment also serves as a factor shaping the role, leading police (as Katz, 1974, contends) to deal with the public in a cautious, distrustful, and violent manner. The law is a framework, as well as a tool, for order maintenance and for the role of the police, e.g., see Roby's comments on the problems of enforcement of the "patron clause" of the New York State prostitution laws (Roby, 1974). The significance of geographical and other differences between communities has also been described (e.g., Ward, 1975). Some have questioned, for instance, whether the police function in the big city can be the same as in the small community. The character of the police subculture itself has been described as a factor conditioning the police role (e.g., Buckner and Christie, 1974). The values which characterize many police subcultures, according to Buckner and Christie, are solidarity of group members, a mentality of suspicion, conservatism in both morality and politics, a reluctance to disclose information about their work, and the use of ruses to control situations outside their legal authority. In shaping its formulation of the role of the police, each community must consider its own situation and the environmental factors that impact on the police agency.

That the police role cannot be characterized as confined to law enforcement is well established in the literature, in practice, and by common sense. In the literature, for example, it is reflected in the categorizations that are offered for policing. One of the best known is James Q. Wilson's three categories of policing—the legalistic, the watchman, and the service. There are others. One describes police role expectations as variations on four ideal types—the social agent, the watchman, the law enforcer, and the crime fighter (O'Neill, 1974). Another distinguishes four role types—the tough cop, the rule-applier, the problem-solver, and the crime-fighter (White, 1974). In practice, the proposition that policing cannot be confined merely to law enforcement is suggested by the fact that the majority of police time is taken up by other activities. The percentage of time allocated to law enforcement tasks will clearly vary by time and by place. Knight gives 60 percent for noncriminal matters (Knight 1977); others will give higher figures. In common sense, it is possible to identify noncriminal activities which seem more important for policing than law enforcement. Saving the drowning boy, for instance, would seem more urgent for any police officer than arresting a pickpocket.

The view that police work cannot be seen as confined only to law enforcement would probably excite little interest if it were not for the social service aspect of policing. The "law enforcement *versus* social service" controversy concerning the definition of the police role has been a major issue for some time (e.g., see Gabor and Low, 1975). Police organizational practices tend to emphasize the law enforcement role, and the police are described as experiencing role conflict since much of their time is spent on peacekeeping and because the public demands social services (Johnson, 1972). Some see the non-law enforcement elements as a regrettable interference with "real police work." Knight, for example, comments that the primary goal of the police remains the eradication of crime and disorder. The police, according to his account, neither created nor can they resolve social problems; the role of the police is "to give law with liberty" (Knight, 1977). The appropriate role is described as the prevention of crime, the protection of persons and property, and the enforcement of laws. Police involvement in social problems, according to this view, should be restricted to problem resolution (Solicitor-General of Canada, 1971). Others see social service as an unavoidable and helpful ingredient of the total police function. Thus, one author writes of the social role as meaning police efforts aimed at preventing people from falling into or continuing in criminal activity or in being victimized by criminals (Feraud, 1977). Another can apply the mental health concepts of primary, secondary, and tertiary prevention in the development of a comprehensive law enforcement planning network (Hanewicz and Minick, 1981).

Mention should be made of another characterization of the nature of police work. Egon Bittner also finds the description of police as law enforcers to be unsatisfactory, because they cope with the majority of their problems without invoking the law. For him, the unifying factor is the situationally justified use of force or the threat of the use of force (Bittner, 1975). The role of the police is to address all human problems that do or may require the use or the threat of force—catching a criminal, preventing a suicide, evicting a drunk from a bar, directing traffic, controlling crowds, and settling domestic disputes. Shearing and Leon follow this argument by explaining that the police role should be defined by focusing on aspects of the work that make it unique (Shearing and Leon, 1977). For them, this is police capability and police license. Police capability is the access to physical force and law enforcement; police license is the authority to use these resources.

Project STAR identified thirteen police roles—assisting the criminal justice system and appropriate agency personnel; building respect for law and the criminal justice system; providing public assistance; seeking and disseminating knowledge and understanding; collecting, analyzing, and communicating information; managing cases; assisting personal and social development; displaying objectivity and professional ethics; protecting the rights and dignity of individuals; providing humane treatment; enforcing the law impartially; enforcing the law situationally; and maintaining order (Chamelin, 1978). Moore describes the work in terms of two functions. One is law enforcement, and the other is peacekeeping. The former emphasizes the crime fighter; the latter places emphasis on crime prevention and the problem-solver (Moore, 1978). The Patrolmen's Benevolent Association of New York once issued a publication entitled *The 1001 Hats of Officer Jones,* emphasizing the variety and number of police tasks.

Three observations can be made about this variety of classifications. First, each is useful in its own way if it adds insight to our understanding of the police mission. For example, it has been suggested that Wilson's categories (law enforcement, order maintenance, and service) should be replaced, being seen as the proactive, reactive, peacekeeping, and service roles (Teaseley, 1978). Both versions have utility. Second, each classification has the limitations of generality. An expansion in the police role in crime prevention, primarily by utilizing crime prevention specialists in the greater application of defensible space and similar concepts, has been suggested (Meadows, 1979), for example. The classifications do not speak to such levels of detail. Third, the categorizations constitute excellent descriptions of the major "processes" of policing. Law enforcement, order maintenance, and service are processes. This tells us that "law enforcement" is to be produced, for example; but it does not specify how much—unless we assume a quantity such as perfect law enforcement, as much as possible, etc.

This account of ideas in the literature on the police function should be viewed as highly selective. For example, references have not been made to the extensive specialist literature on the role of the police in respect to particular functions—domestic crises, juvenile problems, crime prevention and schools, child abuse, rape, white-collar crime, sudden infant deaths, pollution control, racial conflict, alcohol-related traffic offenses, prosecutions of offenders, traffic engineering, strikes in industry, severe weather alert planning, international functions, law enforcement intelligence, skid-row people, terrorism, auto thefts, landlord-tenant disputes, and so on. References to the conclusions of several important committees have been omitted—to the American Bar Association standards, for example. Reference has not been made to the literature on the police function in other countries. A number of striking, although operationally unhelpful, references have also been excluded. It has been argued, for example, that the police and public perceptions of the police role in society have been "moralized" to avoid recognizing the police role in maintaining social class barriers (Fischer–Kowalski *et al.*, 1976). Others stress the political role of the police (Bunyan, 1976). Yet others describe the police in society as basically repressive (Center for Research on Criminal Justice, 1977). On the other hand, selected elements of the mainstream of sociological thinking on the subject have been included.

A SOCIO-ECONOMIC VIEW

A socio-economic view of the function of policing is offered here as a supplement to the sociological descriptions that, as we have seen, abound. Let us ask a simple question— When producing output, what should a rational police department wish to achieve? The answer, although equally simple, underscores the complexity of police policy-making and administration.

A difficulty of defining the outputs of public enterprises is widely recognized. Some economists strive to define single outputs for organizations under analysis. Summers models public schools as single-product firms producing higher test scores (Summers, 1977, 1979), for instance; but she recognizes that schools also produce other outputs like socialization, custodial skills, improved earnings in later life, and screening. In analyzing prisons, Witte identifies "confined days" as a single output (Witte, 1979). Others describe multiple outputs, e.g., Conrad and hospitals (Conrad, 1980), and Getz and libraries (Getz, 1980). Some prefer to view public enterprise outputs as "intermediate." Thus, Witte describes "confined days" as intermediate in the production of incapacitation, punishment, rehabilitation, and deterrence (Witte, 1979). Conrad describes the products of hospitals (e.g., outpatient services, hotel services for patients) as inputs to health (Conrad, 1980).

Police organizations can well be viewed as single-product enterprises, producing "order maintenance service" in reference to socio-economic activity at specific geographical locations. This subsection, using this simplifying but realistic assumption, comments on the conception of a two-directional relationship among order maintenance service (the output of policing), order (the effect of policing and other productive processes), and the socio-economic character of society, and the relation between order maintenance service and location.

Viewing police organizations as single-product enterprises, several stages of intermediate outputs should nevertheless be recognized. At a level below final, for example, it can be argued (although others have not described the situation in these terms) that major intermediate outputs such as the following may be identified—prevention, situation management, and confidence building. Prevention would include items such as preventive patrol and the deterrent effect of criminal investigative activity. Situation management would include responding to disorderly situations (e.g., criminal, traffic, and other) as well as controlling crowds and disturbances. Confidence building would include activities designed primarily to induce a public feeling of safety. At an "earlier" stage of production, another set of intermediate outputs may be described as consisting of patrol, criminal investigation, support and auxiliary services (e.g., see O. W. Wilson, 1978). An even less aggregated description may consist of traditional preventive patrol, casual clothes patrol, stake-out activity, team policing, preliminary investigations, follow-up investigations, crime laboratory services, records administration, jail management, and automobile management.

Police organizations are here understood, then, as single-product firms. In this case, activities such as those noted above are seen as intermediate outputs in the production of a homogeneous product—order maintenance service. For other purposes, of course, the alternative view of police organizations as multi-product organizations can be adopted. Police output (where OM = order maintenance service and OM_n = a type of such service) is then seen as represented by the vector OM $= (OM_1, OM_2, \ldots OM_n)$.

A distinction is drawn here between the terms "order" and "order maintenance service." "Order" is understood to describe a condition of society, an effect (it is assumed) of policing and of other productive processes (e.g., courts) and circumstances (e.g., availability of food supplies). "Order maintenance service," on the other hand, is taken to refer to the output of the police agency as the latter seeks to modify the level of order in society.

"Order" is understood to concern the relationship between people and goods, as this seems to be the common understanding of the concept. Thus, police agencies, intent on achieving a level of order at particular locations, provide order maintenance service concerned to create and/or maintain the quality of relationships among people and between people and goods. As noted above, numerous intermediate activities (many unrelated to law enforcement) are required for such an output. As examples, police agencies are concerned with interdicting some criminal code infractions concerning interpersonal behavior (like murder, rape, and assault) as well as noncriminal disorderly relationships (such as may occur in domestic disturbances). They are concerned about the relationships between people and private goods (e.g., burglary and larceny). They are also concerned about relationships between people and public goods, such as the natural environment. Examples include interdicting despoliation of natural resources, as well as protecting people from natural phenomena such as tornadoes.

It is argued that a two-directional relationship exists among order maintenance service (the product of policing), order (the effect of policing and of other factors), and the socio-economic character of society. Order level impacts on socio-economic character, for example; and the former is a function in part of the latter. The influence of order on socio-economic activity can be illustrated by recalling the types of economic enterprise typically seen (U.S. data) in areas of different order levels. Higher order areas, for instance, may have sidewalk cafes, specialty shops, doctors' offices, indoor shopping malls, pharmacy delivery services, expensive restaurants, and elegant hotels. In lower order areas are bus stations, pawn shops, pizza shops, used car lots, pool halls, laundromats, gambling operations, sidewalk peddlers, fencing activities, and gas stations closed at night. Other things being equal, different kinds of economic activity require particular order levels. Conversely, different types of economic activity contribute to various order levels—in turn, influencing demand for order maintenance service. Some economic enterprises provide more theft opportunities, for example; and some busi-

nesses attract more disorderly customers than others (e.g., por-
nography stores *versus* boutiques in London's Soho).

Order maintenance service cannot be produced and order
cannot be maintained except in relation (not only to concrete
socio-economic relationships but also) to location. "Order
maintenance service" must be "transported" to its consumption site before its production has been completed—just as the
manufacture of a private sector service is incomplete until it
has been transported to its market place. Much order maintenance service will be manufactured at the consumption site,
e.g., by the presence of a police officer; the officer must therefore be transported on the site. Much may be manufactured
elsewhere (e.g., the deterrent effect of a central government's
action on a potential violator at the site); but it is easy to argue
that the "manufacture" must then be transported to the site.
Police resources distribution is, in this view, a matter of production; order maintenance service production has not been
completed until it has been allocated.

Two footnotes should be added about "location." First,
location should be interpreted to include the dimension both
of place and time. Second, order maintenance is a service supplied to individuals. But it is a service supplied to individuals
(or their property) as they occupy locations and in respect to
different socio-economic relations. A more helpful view may
be to conceive of order maintenance service as provided to
locations, which may or may not be occupied by people or
their property. In this situation individuals may in a day
occupy several locations—working here, playing there, and
living in yet another place. The order level that they enjoy
(and demand) may differ among locations.

IMPLICATIONS

The first section of this chapter described views on the
general character of police service. The second indicated that
the volume of order required in particular communities varies

in accordance with the socio-economic character of the neighborhood, and that there is a two-way relationship between order maintenance service (the output of policing), order level (the effect of policing and other factors), and the socio-economic character of communities. This is not an argument for a differential treatment of people—that is repugnant to the present writer. But it is an argument for realistic planning.

Realistic planning begins with the neighborhood. It asks what we want, and need, for that neighborhood in view of its socio-economic nature and prospects. It asks what alternative actions will require in terms of total resources. It looks at the needs of all the neighborhoods, examines the available resources, and then prioritizes resource allocation and policies in order to obtain the best results for the whole community. The available resources are not solely police personnel. They are all the other ingredients that are necessary for order enhancement and that the police agency can induce other agencies and individuals to contribute.

Overall jurisdiction-wide statements of mission for the police do have a value in giving very general shape and direction to the character of the police service. But goal-formulation will hardly be realistic if it speaks only about the nature of policing, and says nothing about the character of the community to be maintained or realized. More precisely, realistic goal-formulation should be based on the varying characters of the constitutent communities. The alternative is the continued encouragement of a process approach to police service, an invitation to bad politics.

PART III

Policy Leadership

"Love your neighbor but be careful of
your neighborhood."
HAY

"To say that private men have nothing
to do with government is to say that
private men have nothing to do with
their own happiness or misery."
CATO

CHAPTER 6

New Community Approach

Communities wishing to come to grips with their crime problems need to adopt a fresh approach to their police agencies, just as urgently as police agencies need to utilize new approaches in relating to their communities. Gone would be the pretense of a politics–administration dichotomy. In its place would be a more open style of police policy-making and administration. The new form of police agency requires a genuine two-way policy interaction between the communities (represented by their elected officials) and the police institution—a new contract that will facilitate order enhancement. Both the politician and the professional must execute their policy leadership responsibilities if the advantages of the new form of police institution are to be realized. This chapter addresses this relationship from the viewpoint of the community; the next takes the vantage point of the agency.

Expressed in mechanistic terms, establishment of the new form of police agency would necessitate two major avenues of policy leadership, two sets of meaningful involvement, by elected officials. The first would be in the development of longer- and short-term plans for order enhancement in the community. The character of these plans was noted in the previous chapter. Such plans would be developed at the initiative of the police agency and in consultation with elements in the community; but elected officials would have a policy leadership responsibility in ensuring the adequacy and relevance of such plans. The second would be in evaluating police programmatic activity in terms of the goals in the various plans. Again, elected officials would have the policy leadership responsibility of ensuring the meaningfulness of such evaluations—of making sure that they rise above the current level of the annual reports, chock full as they are with traditional crime data and other filler information, now produced by many police agencies.

In planning and evaluating, it is difficult for agencies to avoid slippage into meaningless paper-shuffling exercises: the advantages of sinking into sham are very real for both the bureaucrat and the politician. Clearly, there is a cost-benefit advantage for communities to invest financial resources in whatever consulting and full-time staff are necessary to develop and monitor the planning and evaluation system: the investment could be recouped rapidly. Clearly the police agency should be expected to work over the years in improving such systems. But equally clearly, the problems of creating appropriate planning and evaluation systems, while significant and related, pale beside the danger of bureaucratic atrophy. Beyond the mechanistic terms, the new form of police agency requires elected officials with the capability, energy, and will to provide stimuli helpful in counteracting this natural tendency to atrophy.

The new community approach in policy leadership should focus on opening up the police agency. Planning and evaluation systems without this emphasis would soon wither and lose meaning. For too long, police agencies and other governmental agencies have been consumed by process considerations. Even here some may be anxious to read the description and specifications for the planning and evaluation systems. That is a trap. It is more critical to concentrate on the contributions, the stimuli, that the politician should bring in opening up the police agency so that it can work effectively for the community. This chapter describes two such pressures or stimuli that are necessary. In doing so, it incidentally provides further insight into police resources allocation decision-making.

PROFIT-MAKING BURDEN

Scratch a police chief and you will find a bureaucrat. This is not to say that many are not dedicated, fine public servants—working long hours, making hard decisions, experiencing severe work stress, and facing the ever-present possibility of being fired (or retired). But it is to contend that, above all, the police administrator is a time-server, a place-holder. As a time-server, his life is brief: the average police chief serves for some two and a half years. As a place-holder he is usually required to stay out of trouble, to keep his program and subordinates out of severe difficulties, to ensure that disorder does not worsen unacceptably to the public and politicians, and not to cause his political superiors too many serious problems. But the police administrator is not required to enhance order in the community: he does not have the burden of making a programmatic profit.

Let us rush to add that the fault lies, not with the police chief, but with the community. Police administrators have no positive incentives to make a programmatic profit. They will neither receive merit pay nor enjoy longer service. They are not even charged with the responsibility for enhancing order—merely order maintenance. In fact, police administrators have negative incentives. The reality is that achieving police results can often mean effecting change in operating practices, and the harsher reality facing the reformist chief is that most politicians do not want yet another headache. The negative reward, then, can well be earlier retirement to save the politicians further embarrassment.

Let us also rush to exonerate the politicians in that the public has some unduly simplistic notions of governmental effectiveness and crime control. The phenomenon of the "law and order" politician, talking irrelevancies about controlling muggers, is well known in a number of countries. It is hard for the politician, even if he wishes, to point out that the real law and order issue for the elected official is how to control not the criminal but the police chief. It is how to impose the profit-making burden on the police administrator. Such political talk may lose some elections. But, difficult as it is, the politician must pick up the challenge to educate the public.

With all the cunning and energy of which they are capable, politicians should insist that their police chiefs enhance order—and communities should expect this of their politicians. Here, it is true that what is good enough for General Motors is indeed good for the police institution: the chief officials must be able to prove that they are making progress. In the one case, this progress is measured in terms of monetary profit; in the other, it can be described as a programmatic profit. You do tend to get what you ask for; and here the community must ask the politician speaking on crime control to be judged on his creativity. The creativity should lie in creating incentives and disincentives to effective order enhancement. Pay and tenure have already been mentioned: the creative politician will surely advance others.

NEW MODES OF THOUGHT

The value of an open institution is that its effectiveness is increased by exposure to fresh modes of thought, new ways of conceiving old problems. The tragedy of the closed police institution is that it fails to encourage unusual insights: it tends to the uncreative and the moribund, and to tradition and the well-trodden. For insight into such characteristics, see

the accounts of the struggles of the reformist police administrators (e.g., Murphy, 1977). Because new modes of thought
have the potential for realizing positive crime control results,
it is suggested that a major policy stimulus that the elected
official should strive to transmit to the police agency, in the
planning and evaluation activity, is an insistence on fresh
perspectives.

The President's Commission on Law Enforcement and
Administration of Justice in 1967 described America as being
in a war on crime. To those who like the image (and there are
many who deprecate the metaphor), let us ask three questions.
Is the war being won? Are existing modes of thought proving
adequate for the task? Can bureaucrats be relied upon to produce new ideas if the community and the elected officials do
not place a premium on them?

Let us illustrate the new perspective, observing the
insights that its use can bring. The case selected is police
resources allocation decision-making, and the example is the
insights that can be gained from a new vantage point—that of
Economics.

For this purpose, let us focus on three aspects of the economics literature and see how it provides a context for our
thinking about police resources allocation decision-making.
The first is writing on non-market decision-making undertaken without special reference to criminal justice or law
enforcement; it describes economic models of public bureau
behavior. The second covers economic analyses of criminal
justice activity, and the third deals with economics writings
specifically on law enforcement resources distribution.

On Non-Market Decision-Making

Non-market decision-making, as is well known, is now
widely established as an appropriate topic for economic
research; yet it is a mode of thought that most criminal justicians would find foreign when discussing police resources
allocation. Leaving aside Welfare Economics, there has been

an economic journal since 1966—for example—devoted to Public Choice Economics (originally called "Papers on Non-Market Decision-Making") and, in the words of Leiter and Sirkin, "More broadly . . . [the economics of public choice] encompasses all decision-making, whether public or private, that does not involve the conventional type of market analysis" (Leiter and Sirkin, 1979). Earlier, Lionel Robbins explained that "the conception (of economic analysis) we have adopted may be described as analytical. It does not attempt to pick out certain kinds of behavior, but focuses on a particular aspect of behavior. . . . There are no limitations on the subject matter of Economics save this" (Robbins, 1962). Others have utilized this wider view of the character of Economics (e.g., Buchanan, 1967; Tullock, 1969; Breton, 1974; and so on). Gary Becker provided (Becker, 1976) the following examples of the wide applicability of economic analysis (and it is particularly appropriate to quote Becker in view of his influence, noted earlier, in attracting the interest of many economists to criminal justice issues)—evolution of language (Marschak, 1965), church attendance (Azzi and Ehrenberg, 1975), capital punishment (Ehrlich, 1975), the legal system (Posner, 1973; Landes, 1974), the extinction of animals (Smith, 1975), and the incidence of suicide (Hammermesh and Soss, 1974). As another example, Becker himself has applied economic analysis to marriage (Becker, 1973).

Microeconomic concepts and techniques have been applied to a wide variety of functional areas in the public sector. Conrad has done so for hospitals, for example (Conrad, 1980); Getz has analyzed fire departments (Getz, 1979) and libraries (Getz, 1980); and Summers has studied public education (Summers *et al.*, 1977, 1979). It is clear from such studies that basic economic tools can provide helpful insights into issues in specific elements of the public sector. George Stigler provided an example, noted earlier, when he applied the basic concept of marginal analysis to show that laws should be enforced no more than to the point where marginal benefit equals marginal cost (Stigler, 1970).

The economic models of general public bureau behavior can help in understanding police resources allocation decision-making. It is only recently that economic models of public bureau behavior have been developed. An early, possibly the first, economic study of public agency behavior was that by Van Mises in 1944 (Van Mises, 1944). Three such models are noted here—those offered by Niskanen (Niskanen, 1971), by Migue and Belanger (Migue and Belanger, 1974), and by Orzechowski (Orzechowski, 1977).

Niskanen's model assumes that the public manager is a budget maximizer. Factors such as salary, perquisites, power, patronage, and output are a positive monotonic function of the total budget of the bureau; the ease of managing and of making changes are not. In Niskanen's model, the bureau has unique monopoly advantage, and it exacts the full amount of consumer surplus. The model of Migue and Belanger combines Niskanen's notion of the superior-monopoly power of the bureau via the budgetary process and the view that public managers have preferences for items other than output. Unlike Niskanen's, this model predicts production above minimum costs. The DeAlessi-Parkinson Model, offered by Orzechowski, is similar to that of Migue and Belanger in assuming preference for inputs as well as outputs. Parkinson's assumption is labor preference (Parkinson, 1957), while DeAlessi's assumption is preference for capital (DeAlessi, 1969); Orzechowski assumes a bias for labor. Another example of a utility maximization model is Tullock's (Tullock, 1965).

Considerable work has been undertaken recently in adapting the model of the profit-seeking firm to the public sector. This work has encountered difficulties resulting from the complexities of the public sector situation and from the general state of understanding of public enterprise. The complexities of the situation are illustrated in the following paragraph which considers the goals of public enterprise. The general state of understanding is suggested by reviewing comments by Breton about public sector output. Such considerations place police resources allocation decision-making more firmly in the context of the state of present knowledge. It may also be added in parentheses that this application of the private model to the public situation is being attempted at a time when alternatives to the traditional profit maximization hypothesis have been suggested. For example, Simon has offered profit satisficing (Simon, 1959); Williamson has proposed managerial utility maximization (Williamson, 1964), and Baumol (Baumol, 1959) has suggested sales (or growth of sales) maximization. Marris has defined (Marris, 1964) the firm as an enterprise where managers and owners are distinct; see also Scitovsky, 1943.

Difficulties have been experienced in specifying the goals of public enterprise. Niskanen's view was indicated above, for example. Witte, on the other hand, suggests risk avoidance; and she adds that formal goals of public enterprise "while setting a general tone for a public organization are often seen more as constraints than things to be maximized" (Witte, 1980). The difficulty of specifying goals can also be indicated by recent findings concerning the possible goal for public managers of minimizing the costs of producing public services. As mentioned in Chapter 4, Conrad reports that hospitals minimize costs in the short, but not the long, run (Conrad, 1980). Getz notes that libraries are more inclined to minimize costs than fire departments (Getz, 1979, 1980). Summers suggests that cost minimization is of small importance in public school systems (Summers, *et al.*, 1977, 1979), and Phillips notes that police departments do not effectively cost minimize (Phillips, 1978). Because of such differences, some such as Summers have indicated that, rather than adapting current private sector models, a new theory of production should be sought for the public sector.

The general state of understanding of public enterprise is illustrated here by referring to Breton's comments (Breton, 1974) on the output of governments. Breton began his chapter on "The Output of Governments" by noting that "Our knowledge of the public sector is so scant that we do not even have an accepted definition of the output of governments" (Breton, 1974, p. 16). He then goes on to suggest that "the true outputs of government are policies. . . ." An example he gives is that of police protection. He assumes that police protection is the policy objective, which he further defines as "the probability that one's person and/or one's property will not be attacked by criminals in such a way that when this probability increases the amount of police protection supplied increases and, when the probability falls, it decreases." Later, he explained (Breton, 1978, p. 58) that governments "are seen to be organizations analogous to business firms producing a flow of public policies per time-period." The "public sector produces nothing but public policies; or, alternatively, all the outputs of the public sector are public policies. In other words, where we are considering laws, executive orders, statutes, decrees, ordinances, orders-in-council, rules or other kinds of command pertaining to the expenditure or to the collection of money, to the regulation of persons or of institutions, all are public policies by definition."

Breton's assumption that governmental outputs are nothing but policies does have advantages. It is a simplifying notion, permitting additional insight into aspects of public enterprise. It permits distinction between policy objectives (or goals) and policy instruments (or means of achieving the goals), and it underlines the fact that governments do produce policies. But the difficulty with the assumption lies in the meaning of the term "policy." A definition is not provided in Breton's *The Economic Theory of Representative Government* (despite the statement in the index), and the concept appears to be a catchall.

There is also a need to distinguish between the explicit and the implicit policies of an institution. The explicit policy is the stated policy, rule, law, etc., that is issued by the institution. The implicit policy is the policy implied by the level and nature of service actually provided, the result of both political enactment and bureaucratic implementation. It was the latter which Breton had in mind by the phrase "production of public policies."

Three corollaries follow when imperfect information is assumed—as in the real world. First, it is possible for a governmental agency not to know the nature of its output as here defined, its implied policy. Second, it is possible for a governmental agency to produce different outputs as defined in different places and not to be aware of this. For example, the existence of a bureaucrat with responsibility for an area and with a dislike for a particular ethnic group may result in the production of a discriminating output in that area; and a different situation may obtain in another area. Third, several equally valid interpretations of the governmental output may be possible in some circumstances. For example, take the above case of the bureaucrat with responsibility for an area and with a dislike for a particular ethnic group. One explanation is that the government has the policy objective in area A of producing X and the policy objective in area B of producing Y. Another version is that the government is concerned to produce the product, with no policy objective relating to variations. And so on. In these circumstances, the value of utilizing a term like "policies" may be questioned. If governmental output is to be conceived as implied policy, perhaps another word would be appropriate; maybe a totally contrived word with no previous associations. If output is to be conceived only as explicit policy, then such output (where the final product is conceived as the outcome of both political and bureaucratic activity) is really only input.

It is almost tautological that the production of goods and services necessarily involves the production of either explicit or implicit policies. Private enterprise organizations produce outputs consisting of goods and/or services, for example. Such output necessarily implies policy production. This can be explicit, e.g., maximization of profits. It can be implicit, e.g., the poor may not consume truffles daily. The notion of services is very close to that of policies as used by Breton. For instance, Breton gives as some examples of public policies— pest control and space exploration. It is not clearly more useful to define "pest control" as a policy (to control pests); the same with space exploration. And so too with police protection, which Breton gives as the policy output of police.

Breton's comparison of government to business "producing a flow of public policies per time-period" appears problematic when considering a public agency like a police department. If we are to suppose that the output of a police agency is public protection, it is difficult to conceive of a flow of police protections per time-period. The notion of a single unchanging output seems to violate the notion of output. The idea that a police agency will produce more than one such output per time-period suggests that it is more helpful to view police agencies as producing levels of service. It seems of limited utility, without changing the common meaning of the term, to think of such levels as "policy." The net effect of the criticism may be taken to confirm Breton's original statement concerning the scantiness of our knowledge of the public sector.

On Criminal Justice

The economics literature on criminal justice issues has grown in recent years, and it is now substantial. A 1974 bibliography of the *Economics of Crime and Corrections* (American Bar Association, 1974) contained 479 references, for example. A 1978 bibliography (Eskridge, 1978), as another example, contains entries under the headings of general considerations in the economics of criminal justice; corrections; cost-benefit analysis; costs of crimes; drugs, econometrics and statistics; economics of crime; income, employment, and crime; juveniles; law enforcement allocations; organized crime; property and economic crimes; and systems analysis of crime.

Studies have been conducted on a large number of issues in the economics of crime and the criminal justice system. For example, interest has been shown in the environmental correlation of crime (e.g., Harris, 1980; Baer, 1979; Brown, 1979; Georgia State Crime Commission, 1977; and Poole, 1973). But a major theme and perhaps the most useful contribution to an understanding of criminality has been the perspective of writers on the economics of crime, following Becker's model, that criminals are rational, utility maximizers (e.g., Sullivan, 1973;

Rottenberg, 1973; Austin, 1978). Guided by the same considerations as others in legitimate occupations, criminals are
described as calculating the relative net gain from investment
of available resources in illegitimate, as opposed to legitimate,
activity (e.g., see Becker, 1968). At a minimum, revival of such
a view can be taken as useful in that it supplements the sociological explanations of criminality.

Founded on this perspective of criminality, a variety of
general publications and rigorous studies have appeared in
recent years on criminal justice policymaking and on the allocation of criminal justice resources. Illustrative of the general
publications are those noted in this paragraph by Cloninger
and Anderson. Illustrative of the more rigorous are those
noted below by the Hoover Institution, Sedgewick, Heinecke
(also of the Hoover Institution), and Hellman. Cloninger's
publication (Cloninger, 1975) is a textbook on the economics
of criminal behavior and the criminal justice system; for example, it attempts to show how a community can decide the
amount of resources to be allocated to crime control. Anderson's book (Anderson, 1976) analyzes the literature viewing
crime control as a subject of applied welfare economics. It
should be underscored that these two are merely illustrations;
there certainly are others (e.g., McPheters and Stronge, 1975,
a collection of 24 articles concerning the economics of crime
and the criminal justice system). In fact, the literature is wide
enough to have given rise to critiques of the use of economic
analysis in exploring the criminal justice system (e.g., see
Bowers, 1975).

The Hoover Institution, through its Center for Econometric Studies of the Justice System, has produced a number of
analyses of the criminal justice system and policy-making. In
1978, the Institution—with the author remaining anony-
mous—developed an econometric model (Hoover Institution,
1978) relating the expected monetary returns from legal and
illegal activities to labor supply and the property crime level,

and it applied the results to criminal justice policy-making. For example, it pointed out that employment elasticities suggested that policies intended to increase employment will reduce property crimes only if they decrease the long-term employment rate. Sedgewick's study (Sedgewick, 1978) is a doctoral dissertation examining the advantages and limitations of utilizing a welfare economics, rather than a sociological, approach to criminal justice planning. Heinecke's publication (Heinecke, 1978) presents an econometric model of legal and illegal labor supply and explores issues such as the effect of modifications on criminal justice variables. The model estimates the degree of substitution and complementarity between combinations of activities, in addition to participation levels, in response to variations in expected returns and costs. It also allows measures for assessing the effects of changes in such variables as arrest and conviction rates, and sentencing practices. Hellman presents a simultaneous systems approach to analyze the interactions between the urban public sector and urban crime (Hellman, 1979). She offers an econometric model consisting of a system of five equations— a supply of criminal offenses function, a law enforcement production function, a police services demand function, a city revenue function, and a city property value function. Again, this listing of studies is intended for illustrative purposes. This can be underscored by noting the eleven prototypes of previous modeling that are critiqued in Hellman's publications—those by Becker, Katzman, Blumstein and Larson, Orsagh, Single Equation Empirical, Phillips and Votey, Ehrlich, Greenwood and Wadycki, McPheters and Strange, Wilson and Boland, and Hellman and Naroff.

On Law Enforcement Resources Deployment

In his 1970 study of the distribution of police resources in the cities of Chicago and Los Angeles, Giertz concluded that "probably the most important conclusion to be gained from this analysis is that general statements concerning the distribution of police are extremely difficult to make" (Giertz, 1970, p. 66). This view remains valid.

Yet, considerable work has been done on issues of police resources allocation. For example, the public expenditure literature contains extensive treatment of the determinants of police expenditures (e.g., see McPheters and Stronge, 1974), and of the effects of police expenditures (e.g., see Pogue, 1975); there is a lengthy literature relating variations in public spending to various environmental factors (e.g., see Borcherding and Deacon, 1972) and on the demand for public goods (e.g., see Bergstrom and Goodman, 1973). Substantial work has also been undertaken in modelling police production. In *An Economic Analysis of the Provision of Police Services*, for example, Emerson presented an economic model for the provision of police services (Emerson, 1972). In 1978, Llad Phillips published his *Factor Demands in the Provision of Public Safety* (Phillips, 1978). In the same year, as another example, Darrough and Heinecke presented their *Multi-Output Translog Production Cost Function* (Darrough and Heinecke, 1978).

Issues significant for police resources distribution have been addressed in the economics literature. An example is the issue of the character of returns to scale in policing (e.g., see Walzer, 1972; Darrough and Heinecke, 1978, etc.). Beyond this, however, the economic literature contains little at the intra-agency level on the distribution of police resources. Giertz's publication *An Economic Analysis of the Distribution of Police Patrol Forces* (Giertz, 1970) was an exception. A main thrust of this research was to examine the relationship between the geographical distribution of the patrol force and a variety of demographic and other environmental variables. Other studies, while not described by their authors as economic analyses, have been undertaken on similar lines. For example, Saladin undertook such a study for Columbus, Ohio, in his 1980 doctoral dissertation in the Department of Management Sciences at Ohio State (Saladin, 1980). The contribution of such intra-agency studies to an understanding of police deployment may be viewed as marginal. For example, Giertz's main finding was that there is a high positive correlation between the level of criminal activity and police deployment! Saladin found correlations with population, density, affluence, and building vacancy.

Some valuable insights have been offered. In the same year that Giertz commented on the difficulty of making general statements on police distribution, for example, George Stigler published an article, "The Optimum Enforcement of Laws" (Stigler, 1970). In terms of economic theory, the basic notion in Stigler's article was elementary; in terms of legal and criminal justice theory, explicit application of the notion to the enforcement of laws was radical. Stigler's observation was that a particular law should be enforced only up to the point where marginal social cost equals marginal social benefit. As another example, consideration may be given to Darrough's and Heinecke's study of the *Multi-Output Translog Production Cost Function* (Darrough and Heinecke, 1978). In that study Darrough and Heinecke "adopted the economic model of an optimizing firm as a framework for characterizing the production structure of a sample of medium-sized U.S. law enforcement agencies" (Darrough and Heinecke, 1978, p. 299). Among the hypotheses tested in that study is that of cost minimization, and the authors concluded "that, at least in (their) sample, the decisions of police administrators seem to be inconsistent with cost minimization." Llad Phillips reports a similar conclusion (Phillips, 1978).

The reader is left to judge whether the general point has been made. The new form of police institution, thinking about problems like resources allocation, must be alert to new perspectives. Does review of an "unfamiliar and strange" literature like that of economics add to an understanding of police resource allocation decision-making for those to whom such a literature is new? Clearly, it does.

IMPLICATIONS

The policy leadership role of the community, acting through its elected officials, is critical for establishing the purposive, open type of police institution that is necessary if crime is to be effectively controlled. In participating in the planning and evaluation process for the new form of police agency, reliance must be placed on the politician for establishing the profit-making burden on the police administrator and for insisting on police receptivity to new modes of thinking. Without such stimuli, the planning and evaluation processes are likely to deteriorate into bureaucratic exercises that achieve little.

Meaningful policy leadership, expressed through planning and evaluation shared between the politician and the professional, is likely to diminish the opportunity for bad politics. But the fear of bad politics should not be permitted to drive out good policy leadership. Policing is far too important to be left entirely to the police chief.

Could local governments acting alone bring off this new community approach? While surely a possibility, the chances would be increased if the federal and state governments—particularly the federal—provided an improved climate of support. The federal government could do so by refocusing its current police research, leadership and educative activities—functions now carried out by agencies like the National Institute of Justice, and the Bureau of Criminal Justice Statistics—to develop model approaches. The state government could also exercise leadership and educative roles through its power of the purse, training, and other activities. How a particular governmental level discharges the responsibility is a matter of politics at the particular place and time, although there are advantages in establishing a Presidential (or Gubernatorial) Commission on the subject every decade or so. The point is that however it is done the responsibility is there. Policing is far too important—even though it should remain at the community level—to be left entirely to local governments.

CHAPTER 7

A New Managerial
Approach

To control crime, a new form of police institution is needed that is purpose-oriented, outgoing to the environment, and creative; the new managerial approach is to seek this new form. The three major capabilities that cumulatively characterize the new form of police institution were described in the first chapter. Concerning purpose, it is the capacity for developing—in consultation with other public and private agencies—plans for order enhancement. Concerning outgoingness or openness to the environment, it is the capacity for mobilizing and leading agencies and individuals to achieve the improved order level. Concerning creativity, it is the capacity for utilizing research results and new perspectives in achieving the other two capabilities. This chapter comments on these three capabilities—providing an account of the new managerial approach, that new direction for police management that can be expected to work with the new community approach to give us crime control and the other benefits of the new form of police agency. The first section of this chapter describes purpose-orientation, providing an account of a budgeting method of police resources allocation decision-making. The second comments on openness in both policy-making and implementation, and the third discusses creativity.

But first let us comment on tilt. A madman, obsessed with a passion for police and police work, might be disbelieved— but forgiven—for feverishly imagining a systematic conspiracy to suppress police effectiveness. Society has designed police work, the madman may suppose, in the image of the typical person it recruits to police work. He would observe that many police managers and many police officers are no more than amateurs in professionals' clothing. He would note that the police personnel system is designed essentially to attract mere high school graduates, to keep them in their home locales all through their working lives by civil service and pension provisions, and to draw the ranking officers almost exclusively from among those who have slowly wended their way up through the ranks. The madman would suppose that, done at its highest level, police management and police work can rise even above the professional to almost the priestly or ministerial level. Now, he would fulminate, police are little more than "construction workers in blue;" police managers are frequently only foremen. The madman would also note the special disabilities in the United States, which, he would claim, has no "police system"—merely a mushroom proliferation of agencies, many too small for effectiveness. What are the basic operating principles of policing? And he would answer—tradition, on your own, maintain control, cover yourself, get by. What is the typical management style?—management-by-crisis. What characterizes the planning function?—grantsmanship, short-term limited skills. What describes a police chief?—local person, risen through the ranks, minimal management and criminal justice training. Thank goodness that the madman's conspiracy delusion is unfounded! But, to the extent that the community and the elected officials can "tilt the deck" to favor the real professionals and professionalism in the police service, the more likely is the new police managerial approach to be realized—the more likely is the new form of police agency to be established (see Stead, 1981, for comments on police leadership).

The options for tilting the deck range from the minimal, through the radical, to the relatively impossible; and communities must take steps consistent with local needs and circumstances. As the years progress, the impossible is likely to come increasingly within the realm of the possible. At the minimal end, options for strengthening the professional element in the police service would include financial and pay differential support of criminal justice education for police personnel, civilianization of key positions in the police agency such as planning heads, and encouragement of working relations between the agency and other community institutions like universities. At the more radical end, options can be pursued that seek to infuse the police institution with a professional approach. The madman, speaking again, may shock us by proposing a merging of the police and the prosecutorial agencies to establish the prosecutor as police chief; providing for dual levels of entry, similar to the military system; and requiring college degrees (as the President's Commission on Law Enforcement and Administration of Justice recommended in 1967) for admission to the police service. In seeking the appropriate incentive for the new managerial approach in the police agency, the elected official must not ignore a powerful option at the minimal end of the range— that of hiring a far-sighted, energetic, and truly professional police chief, able to give a commitment of working toward establishing the new form of police agency.

PURPOSE-ORIENTATION

Continuing reformulation and evaluation of purpose—in partnership with elected officials—is a primary element of the new managerial approach, of the new form of police agency. Police agencies have always had, it has been noted, a general

sense of mission. Charles Reith analyzed British police principles (Reith, 1952) as they emerged in Robert Peel's New
Police of London in 1829. The first principle, he said, was "to
prevent crime and disorder as an alternative to the repression
of crime and disorder by military force and severity of punishment." In Los Angeles today it is "to protect and serve."
Consistent with this overall mission, it has been indicated that
police agencies have become dominated by process: the
resources allocation example was explained in detail. The new
form of police agency takes this general acceptance of purpose
a step further, specifying that achievement of purpose must
be based on a continuing process of planning and policy formulation—of definition of purposes, subpurpose and priorities, of evaluation of achievements, and of reformulation of
plans in view of such feedback.

Beyond this, the new form of planning has four major
characteristics. It is open, reaching out to other public agencies and to private institutions. This was described earlier as
the capacity for working with other institutions in developing
workable purpose, plans, and policies. It is proactive. This
term, much overworked and abused in police management, is
here used in the sense of working for programmatic profit, of
anticipating problems aggressively. It centers on solving
problems, rather than merely coping with incidents. It is subject to community evaluation. Examples of this new type of
output were offered in Chapter 1 in the outline of the new
form of police agency.

In an ideal world, the police administrator would recruit
and select personnel qualified to do this difficult and creative
work, and he would establish systems to facilitate plan and
policy formulation. In the real world, he is limited by the
quality of personnel currently dominating his system, and he
faces the difficulty that his employees are often unsuited for
effective planning. In the real world, he often feels trapped
by the weight of existing systems and practices. Paramilitarism and the career system tend toward process, for example,
and these may be nuts too hard for him to crack, even if he

worked to do so. Hampered by the inertia of immovable humans and systems, the administrator is clearly reduced to patch and stitch. He must struggle on a piecemeal basis to raise the educational level of his officers, strive to bring in qualified civilians, chip away at organizational impediments, and create more and more purpose-oriented systems. The approach can only be incremental.

Focusing here on the continuing function of purpose formulation and reformulation, let us examine an example of the type of purpose-oriented system building that is required for the new form of police agency. Let us take the case of police resources allocation decision-making, drawing particularly on the experience of the New York City Police Department. This case tells much about the new managerial approach; it also indicates directions for police resources allocation decision-making.

Police resources allocation decision-making, clearly, is a form of budgeting that uses as the numeraire not money but employees. Such decision-making determines the volume of scarce resources, the percentage of departmental and other effort, that will be invested in particular activities at specified locations at defined times. Viewed as such, resources allocation decision-making in a police agency should be treated as a form of budgeting—or to use a more modern term, as a type of planning–budgeting.

Three critical corollaries follow this understanding of resources allocation decision-making. First, such decision-making cannot achieve optimal results unless it is linked intimately with purposes and plans. The earlier comments in Chapter 3 about ends and means in budgeting (about PPBS, MBO, and ZZB) will come to mind. The quest for a simple police resources allocation formula was bound to fail, just as the search for a magic formula for allocating money is bankrupt. There is no process that can relieve the budgeteer from the chore of analyzing and prioritizing purposes as a preliminary to allocating resources. Second, such decision-making will also be lacking to the extent that it is not firmly wedded to results analysis. Purpose and policy formulation depend largely on evaluation of circumstances and program results, feedback useful for adjusting the subsequent volley of activity. Third, resources allocation that confines itself to deployment within existing programs—a process defined in the first chapter as Micro-Resources Allocation—should be recognized as the narrow activity that it is. It is parallel to budgeting that starts with the premise that all programs will be retained essentially as they are.

For 1972, the New York City Police Department introduced and used the Manpower Allocation Review System (MARS). It is an example of a budgeting, purpose-oriented approach to police resources allocation decision-making. It does differ from the type of planning that should be expected in the new form (after all, the NYPD was not, and is not, a new form of police agency) in that it was closed within the police agency and it was neither as proactive nor as sophisticated as it could have become. But it was a beginning that could have been developed over time into a full-fledged system with all the required characteristics. Not because of any dissatisfaction with the system but for extraneous reasons (e.g., the departure of Commissioner Patrick V. Murphy, other interests for the present writer), the beginning was a one-time use. It was a single, feeble harbinger—but a harbinger indicating the possibility of change and of the purpose-oriented approach that might be. It was forerunner of what must come.

In brief, the MARS system consisted of scrutinizing each functional activity of the police agency. A budget board, armed with analytical information in staff papers, sat and reviewed each "request" for manpower "funds." This board consisted of the principal officials of the Department—the Police Commissioner, the First Deputy Commissioner, and the Chief Inspector (now Chief of Operations). The staff work for each review was conducted by the Department's Planning Division; essentially it consisted of a series of options for changing the operation under review. The culmination of the process was a hearing between the Board and the respective commanders, discussing the various programmatic and manpower options.

This is the way that the system was described in the boiler-plate preface to the packages prepared on each of the functional units. "The MARS hearings constitute a means whereby the Police Commissioner and his principal advisors will meet with the respective administrators or commanders to review the manpower allocated to functions within the department. The principal questions to be addressed will be: How are the men being used? Can the manpower level in this function be reduced? Should the complement be increased? What basic changes should be made in current practices in order to optimize manpower utilization?

The preface continued, "It is a system providing for the periodic and comprehensive budgeting of the department's most important resource (manpower), aimed at determining the relative marginal benefits of reassigning manpower among the various functions of the department. A basic element of MARS is the marginal benefit approach. This technique involves identifying the effects of changes (increases and decreases) in the existing complements of units, and in adjusting levels to yield an optimum effect for the entire department. The focus is not on total costs and benefits but on marginal cost-effectiveness. The marginal approach is based on the idea that a number of additional (or less) men in any one unit is unlikely to give the same benefits or results as the addition or subtraction of the same number of men in another unit, and that the department should seek to balance the effectiveness by making marginal changes in the complements of units. This principle has the same validity here as a marginal utility analysis in Economics. In terms of allocating police manpower among units, this approach thus focuses on the effects of changing existing complement levels. What would happen if a particular unit were reduced by a specified number of officers? Would greater or less benefits be secured by transferring the manpower saved to another unit? These are the sort (sic) of questions addressed in the marginal benefit approach.

"Workload, functional relationship and cost-benefit data are utilized in MARS in order to provide information for the marginal benefit approach. The workload technique, for instance, involves identifying the work units by which the work volume of a function or unit can be measured; determining the time required per work unit; projecting the workload of the function or unit for a coming period, and then calculating the number of men required. The functional relationship method is a variation of the workload technique in that it consists of relating staff size to certain factors which are indirect indicators of workload. The measurement of workload is not direct, as in the previous method. Thus one study related the size of the traffic law enforcement group to such factors as the number of billions of miles traveled by traffic within the jurisdiction, congestion (defined as the average number of vehicles per square mile), etc. The cost-benefit method involves calculating total costs, estimating benefits associated with these total costs, and then determining optimum levels in terms of relative cost-benefits. This method centers on total costs and benefits.

The preface continued, "This is the first set of annual hearings conducted as part of MARS. The introduction of the system constitutes a significant step forward by the department in the management of its resources. Because of the newness of MARS, however, difficulties and shortcomings are anticipated primarily in terms of information. The department has a very long way to go in developing an adequate management information system giving data on the current utilization of manpower. Staff work for the current hearings has made a good start. As MARS develops over the years, it is the intention that progress will be made in collecting more sophisticated information and in conducting more extensive analyses."

Let us take an example—the Special Operations Division. The functions of this city-wide division were to "maintain patrol in designated areas during hours of the day when crime or other unusual police hazards require reinforced or specialized patrol in such areas, to provide for the policing of special events and unusual situations requiring police attention of a specialized nature, to maintain a mobile emergency service, to provide for mounted patrol in areas where large crowds congregate, and to assist in crowd control at labor disputes, public assemblages and similar occurrences." The options considered under MARS for the six units of this division were:

- Special Events Squad and Tactical Patrol Force
  Elimination
  Consolidation

- Mounted District
  Elimination
  Reduction
  Redefinition

- Emergency Service Units
  Reassign ambulettes
  Reassign ambulance and medical unit personnel

- Aviation Unit
  Define objectives
  Greater use of helicopters and personnel
  Reduction

- Stakeout Unit
  Reduction
  Transfer to Detective Bureau
  Elimination

- Harbor Patrol Unit
  Transfer the function to another agency
  Reduction in the number of launches
  Reassignment of crewmen

To take another example, the options considered for the eight units of the city-wide Traffic Division were as follows:

- Traffic Education Unit

> *Elimination of traffic education function*
> *Transfer of traffic education function from the Police Department to the Department of Traffic*
> *Transfer of the traffic education function from the Traffic Division to the Community Affairs Division*
> *Replacement of the police officers in the Traffic Education Unit by police trainees*

- Taxi Safety Squad
  > *Elimination*
  > *Reduction and modification of mission*

- Accident Investigation Squad
  > *Transfer of the accident investigation function to the Scientific Research Division or the Detective Division*
  > *Reduce the manhours expended administering the intox drivers tests by implementing the Breathalyzer Test and reduce the number of personnel assigned accordingly*
  > *Expand the functions of the Accident Investigation Squad to include the investigation of all vehicle accidents*
  > *Realign duty charts to have more men available when the demands for service are the greatest*

- Motorcycle District
  > *Redesignate the Motorcle District as the Highway Patrol District and eliminate the use of motorcycles*
  > *Implement One-man Radio Motor Patrol for selected low and medium hazard posts*

- Queens Traffic District
  > *Eliminate Queens Traffic District and assign its functions to the patrol force*
  > *Retain Queens Traffic District and its functions, but reduce its manpower complement*
  > *Retain Queens Traffic District, but eliminate the summons enforcement function and reduce the manpower complement*

- First Traffic District
  > *Removal of summons enforcement function from First Traffic District Office*

- Traffic Units A and B
  Elimination
  Consolidation
  Retention of present structure with reductions in personnel
  Elimination of the summons enforcement function
- Parking Enforcement Squad
  Elimination and transfer of the towing function to the Department of Traffic
  Elimination of the summons enforcement function and a reduction in manpower
  Change the towaway function to a one-man operation with a reduction in manpower
  Civilianization of all nonpolice functions with a reduction in total manpower
  Change in towing procedures.

For each option considered under MARS, the Planning Division prepared supporting material analyzing the alternatives. The following example of the Aviation Unit is provided in the Example. Three features will be noticed. First, a goal of the MARS activity was the long-term effort of working toward greater departmental appreciation and formulation of purpose. Second, even a rudimentary level of analysis can yield substantial results. Third, the utility of proceeding beyond the Micro-Resources Allocation level is clear. In parenthesis, it should be emphasized that no conclusions about the operation of New York's present Aviation Unit should be drawn from data prepared on that unit for 1972.

EXAMPLE
Resource Utilization in the Aviation Unit

AVIATION UNIT

The effect of altering the manpower level in the Aviation Unit can be gauged by considering the present utilization of aircraft and personnel. Neither is being used as much as possible, and, with an adjustment in individual productivity, it would appear that an appropriate reduction in personnel would have no significant effect on the department's overall aviation program.

Detailed information on the current utilization of helicopters and pilots is maintained in the Aviation Unit. The extent to which helicopters are flown can be evaluated by comparison with the manufacturer's estimates of flying capability and other criteria. The amount of flying time done by the pilots can be compared with criteria such as the amount of time they can, and should, fly.

Information on the effects of modifying the manpower level in the Aviation Unit can also be obtained by reviewing the objectives of the aviation function. However, this is complicated by the fact that, beyond general objectives, the precise purposes and techniques of the Aviation Unit have never been developed to the extent that they should be.

OPTIONS

MARS data on the current utilization of helicopters and personnel indicate that the Police Department has three possible major options in strengthening its aviation program, i.e., to define more precisely the objectives, subpurposes, and methods of the Aviation Unit; to obtain greater use from the existing number of helicopters and personnel; to reduce the number of men (and possibly helicopters) in the Aviation Unit. Each of these options is discussed, in turn, below.

DEFINITIONS OF OBJECTIVES

The missions of the Aviation Unit are clear:

a. To perform aerial patrol and conduct traffic, maritime, and other specialized surveys for other units of this department and for other agencies of this city.
b. To provide specialized emergency services, i.e., medical flights, rescues, etc.
c. To enforce pertinent laws applicable to aircraft operations within the city.

To execute its mission, the Aviation Unit undertakes aerial patrol; maritime patrol and rescues; security patrols; rooftop surveys; aerial photography; enforcement of laws relative to aircraft operations; traffic surveys; and medical emergency flights.

Work needs to be done, however, in strengthening the department's plan for utilizing helicopters. The extent of the current utilization is documented in tables appearing in this report (but not included in this book). The productivity results of the 47th Precinct experiment suggest the need particularly to explore further the use of helicopters in general patrol, and suggest the need for better crime data on which to base aviation operations.

This need to refine plans for the use of aircraft in police department operations was also reflected in the statement of the Commanding Officer of the Aviation Unit that "The potential of the helicopter as a law enforcement tool has not yet been fully realized. Precinct crime prevention patrol can probably be expanded. More sophisticated covert nightvision equipment will result in greater utilization of the helicopter in nighttime operations . . ."

BETTER UTILIZATION OF RESOURCES

Data maintained by the Aviation Unit indicates that present aviation equipment and manpower resources are underutilized. This is shown in Tables 5 and 6 (excluded from this publication) showing the number of hours flown by helicopters and pilots during 1971.

Use of Helicopters: The number of hours flown by helicopters of the Aviation Unit can be compared against two standards. The first is an estimate by the manufacturer (Bell Aviation) of the extent to which the helicopter can be utilized. The second is a use rate calculated from the maximum use made of each helicopter during any month, and this is the standard utilized here. The logic of the latter standard, which is lower than the first, is that a helicopter in good repair should be able to fly as much in any month as it does in the month of its maximum utilization.

The amount the helicopters could have flown, if each flew in every month the amount it was utilized in its highest month, was 2753.6 hours higher than was actually flown. To the extent that this analysis is valid, the equivalent of 2.3 helicopters were not utilized.

The following table indicates the maximum flown by each helicopter in any month and the additional hours of possible flying time per annum if each aircraft flew every month as much as it flew in the maximum month.

Plane #	Maximum flown in any month	Additional flying hours possible
1	64.3	396.4
2	82.9	405.6
3	97.8	180.0
4	89.8	472.6
5	69.7	403.6
6	85.9	511.4
7	82.6	384.0

Use of Pilots: The number of hours reported flown by the pilots can also be compared against two standards. The first is the maximum possible number of flying hours identified by the manufacturer's representative. The second is a standard of 80 hours per pilot per month, a figure discussed with the Commanding Officer of the Aviation Unit.

On the more realistic standard of 80 hours per pilot, 4.1 pilots could have flown the helicopters to the extent that they were flown in 1971. Two-man teams would require 8 or 9 pilots. Allowing for exigencies, this figure should be increased to 12 pilots.

Data was not obtained on the use of mechanics. However, it is noted that the Aviation Unit has 1.43 mechanics for every helicopter.

REDUCTION IN PERSONNEL AND AIRCRAFT

Rather than increasing the activity of the AVIATION Unit, an option available to the Police Department is to reduce the number of men per aircraft, and require the same total population.

The manpower levels and assignments reported in November 1971 for the Aviation Unit were:

1 Captain	C.O., rated helicopter pilot
1 Lieutenant	Maintenance supervisor
1 Lieutenant	Training—rated helicopter instructor pilot
3 Sergeants	Supervisors of pilots and mechanics
17 Patrolmen	Rated helicopter pilots
10 Patrolmen	Certified aircraft mechanics
1 Patrolman	Clerical duty
1 Patrolman	Stockroom
6 Patrolmen*	Security (**restricted duty)

A reduction of up to ten patrolmen appears feasible, including some pilots, mechanics, and security personnel.

LEADERSHIP AND OPENNESS

The fundamental significance of an intimate police–community relationship has been recognized, although sometimes forgotten, throughout the modern history of policing. Five of Reith's Peelian principles of law enforcement are on the subject (Reith, 1952). The most eloquent is the principle that "The police at all times should maintain a relationship with the public that gives reality to the historic tradition that the police are the public and that the public are the police; the police are the only members of the public who are paid to give full-time attention to duties which are incumbent on every citizen in the interests of community welfare." Others include the observation that the "ability of the police to perform their duties is dependent upon public approval of police existence, actions, behavior, and the ability of the police to secure and maintain public repect;" another is his statement that the "police must secure the willing cooperation of the public in voluntary observance of the law to be able to secure and maintain public respect."

Enough voices have been raised to emphasize the necessity of close ties between the police and the public, the insufficiency of the efficiency model. The forgetting of the necessity of close ties was encouraged by the application of such innovations as the automobile and the radio; the remembering was facilitated by developments like the civil rights movement and the rising crime rate. The efficiency model still persists in many police agencies, however. Police patrol officers, driving and redriving down main streets for preventive patrol purposes, are encouraged to rush to and through their response to calls for service, so that they can get back "into service" driving down the main streets—as if driving is "in service." In many departments, there is managerial pressure to be "out of service" dealing with a call for no more than an average of thirty minutes.

The openness and leadership of the new form of policy agency goes beyond Peel's position. Peel specified that the police should seek and preserve public favor "in complete independence of policy." The new managerial approach, on the one hand, would agree with him in not seeking (in Reith's words on Peel) merely to cater to public opinion; it would aim for absolutely impartial service to the law; it would have no regard for the justice or injustice of the substance of individual laws, and it would offer "individual service and friendship to all members of the society without regard to their race and social standing." But, on the other hand, the policy-making in the new form of policing would be shared openly with elected representatives, and the police agency woul provide community leadership in inducing organizations, groups, and individuals outside the police department to cooperate in achieving the goals.

As these views run contrary to conventional wisdom, a reminder and a comment are appropriate—the former on policy-making and the latter on openness. The reminder is the distinction, made earlier, between good politics and bad. Good politics is here understood as the community's inputs, primarily through elected officials, to the planning and policy formulation process. Bad politics is viewed as the intrusion, usually in a nonpublic and typically self-interested manner, in the day-to-day activities of police management and operations.

The comment is that much is kept confidential in policing that need not be secret; maintaining the secrecy, in fact, reduces the effectiveness. A comparison can be made here with the physician. In earlier years, the typical physician tended to share little information with the typical patient— the doctor knew best, and there seemed excellent reasons for not involving the patient. Now, the more modern physician will tell all, explain the options, and indicate the course he would like to follow. As medicine becomes even more research-informed, the delightful paradox is that the patient seems to have become more important in the doctor–patient relationship. Policing suffers from the same traditional curse of secrecy. Secrecy is a useful shield for lack of rationale and even for incompetence—in policing no less than in medicine. Of course, some police information must remain confidential. It is easy to list examples from day-to-day operations—information which could hurt or embarrass groups or individuals, information which could permit criminals to evade detection and apprehension, information relating to a prosecution, information which could frustrate the order-enhancement purposes of the agency. But information of policy-making significance—on items concerning resources allocation, for example—need not remain secret. In securing achievement of goals, some sharing of operational data may be necessary. The police manager can become as bold as the physician; he can share many of his secrets.

Let us be more specific and take a sensitive topic like stake-out squads, which are sometimes maintained by very large cities like New York and Los Angeles. As the name implies, the function of such squads is to "stake out" stores that have experienced multiple robberies. Heavily equipped, the officers hide in "blinds" perhaps for twenty or more days—with the hope of intercepting a robbery. When a robbery occurs, the squad attempts to arrest the perpetrators; however, exchange of gunfire and deaths of robbers are not uncommon. Obviously, this is the kind of operation that the police could never delegate to another agency. What kind of information, if made public, about these squads would impede police effectiveness and efficiency? Clearly the publication of operational information like the locations of current stake-outs or the names of stake-out officers would frustrate the process. But beyond this, there is much of policy-making concern that could, and should, be made public. For example, information could well be made available on the costs and benefits of the program, on the relative merits of alternative appoaches, and on the principles and criteria underlying program objectives. On the policy execution level, there is perhaps nothing that should be shared with another agency.

The new managerial approach of openness has risks for the police manager no less than for the physician. In a sense, information shared is power shared, and many of the public think neither realistically nor well on order maintenance issues. Some would add that, for that matter, neither does the public seem to think well on medical or any other issues—and ignorance was once considered a valid argument for the physician being the autocrat. Many citizens know little of crime and policing; many have psychological hangups (of either undue love, or undue hatred, for the authority figure in uniform); and many have critical and analytical faculties ill-developed for serious thinking about public affairs. Asked to think about the criteria underlying use of a stake-out squad, for example, some may well adopt an unbalanced view—single-mindedly either lusting for more robbers' blood or denying the harsh reality that deadly force is unavoidable in some street situations. The manager's working life in an open situation is much harder. But democracies routinely do it where the subject matter is more complex than policing and where the risks are even greater. Foreign affairs, fiscal matters, trade practices, military service—policies on all such subjects are developed openly and democratically under the same circumstances. Many government agencies work closely with, and through, extra-governmental institutions.

Hemmed in by such constraints, the police manager will probably choose an incrementalist approach to greater information sharing, just as for policy-making. Legislatures may choose to be more radical. The current Freedom of Information and Privacy acts have proved useful tools for greater democratization of governmental administration. Following careful and critical analysis of what must be secret, similar provisions could be enacted to open up and govern release of police policy and management information.

The police agency, attempting to provide leadership in mobilizing community resources, must be prepared to do more than exhort. It must rise above the level of such programmatic banalities as Officer Friendly and the typical Community Relations Unit. Such an agency must learn to let go—to let others share in some of the doing. Rather than being merely a "doing" organization, it must work toward becoming a thinking-and-doing agency with the accent on developing creative approaches for community involvement.

Again, it should be stressed that some functions can never be delegated, e.g., stake-out squads.

The madman would suggest that the majority of the complement of a police agency should be community organizers à la Saul Alinsky workers, that police commanders should think of themselves as community developers, and that agencies should explore such innovations as grant-giving to organizations willing and qualified to carry out order-enhancement projects. We need not agree with all the madman thinks, but police agencies should hire some madman to stimulate their creative, planning juices.

A former First Deputy Commissioner of the New York City Police Department told the writer of his reaction when he found out that the Bronx Borough Police Commander was using some of his officers to clean up a canal. "You are the Chief of Police, not the Chief of People," the First Deputy Commissioner reportedly told the borough commander. It is arguable that, in seeking order enhancement, the Borough Commander was in the right. He would have been even more right if he had used his officers to induce other agencies and individuals to work on cleaning up the canal—if his staff had had the capability and mandate to give leadership to other agencies in developing community improvement plans.

CREATIVITY

The key to the new managerial approach, in realizing the type of purpose orientation and openness described here, is the awakening and nurturing of organizational creativity— the encouragement of the application of research, and of new perspectives, in these and in all police activities. The same creativity would also be a feature of the full-fledged professional model, and, emphasizing this, the examples given here also could apply to that model. But the new form of police agency is incomplete without this creativity. As was noted

earlier, it is the cumulative consequence of the three characteristics that distinguishes the new form.

Certainly, realization of this creativity requires the commitment of a substantial quantity and quality of personnel
resources to the planning function. A thinking, creative
agency requires personnel capable of sophisticated analysis
and understanding, and it is not readily apparent why police
agencies should find it more cost-effective to make a smaller
investment in planning than any large profit-conscious corporation like General Motors or L.T.V. But, beyond this, creativity is required in police management; police administration
should be routinely creative, rather than merely routine. Both
these points are discussed below.

Police agencies have improved in this respect in recent
years. But by and large, they stumble along without the
advantages of sufficient planning capability. Let us document
the point by considering crime analysis, a topic where police
planning performance may be expected to be at its most developed. Based on site visits to twenty-two representative police
agencies, the Foundation for Research and Development in
Law Enforcement and Criminal Justice—as part of the
National Evaluation Program—concluded that "There is some
evidence that a sense of the value of information for decision-
making is catching on among police administrators, but, with
notable exceptions, there is no one in the field who appears
to be able to point to specific linkages between crime analysis
activity and goal attainment" (Reinier, 1976). To quote selec-
tively from the same report—"The actual analysis appears to
be primarily pin mapping, or clustering of one type or the
other, although heavy reliance is placed on the 'read and
recall' capability of individuals." "With respect to. . . . the
development of alternate schemes and the results of these
plans, it can only be said that this function is almost non-exis-
tent in the field. On the whole, the entire area of problem
solution and specification of programs remains virgin terri-
tory, still awaiting systematic practical implementation, with
the exception, perhaps, of the New Haven area departments."

And the Foundation's report observed that "Overall, little conclusive evidence was found to substantiate the value of crime analysis as an appropriate function or in what way it should be structured to be cost effective. At nearly every site, representatives were merely speculative about the advantages of crime analysis or indifferent to the subject" (Reinier, 1976). The new managerial approach can hardly be attempted with insufficient planning and research staff in the police agency, both in terms of quantity and quality.

Police managers in the new form of police agency—as in the fully-developed professional model—would be creative information gatherers and analysts on order-enhancement programs and techniques. What works?—when, where, how, and why? What does not work?—where, when, how, and why? Police agencies have done such a creditable public relations job of projecting the appearance of knowledge and competence about crime control that it may be shocking to some, nourished on the capability of literary and television police, to recognize that the cupboard is almost empty. Outside a relatively narrow spectrum, not much has been firmly established about what works and what does not work in on-the-street policing.

If agencies were not so concerned to project an image of being in full control and command, many police officers would not find it so difficult to admit this inside secret either to themselves or to others. Certainly it is not a problem confined to policing; nor is it a problem that makes policing any less important. Alice Rivlin was referring to the managers of all social programs when she wrote of the need for managers to design programs in such a way as to gather evaluative data that would contribute to the development over time of more solid information about program alternatives (Rivlin, 1972). She wrote of the need to gather this information through such methods as natural and systematic experimentation. Rather than being merely a doer, the manager engaged in natural and systematic experimentation would be both a doer and a thinker. He would design his programs systematically in order to gather hard evaluative program data. The police manager must be no less creative and research-oriented.

As an example, for both the professional model and the new form, consider these three facts about corruption. First, corruption is a continuing concern for any police chief. That police work inevitably involves exposure to corruptive influences and that some police officers do succumb (whether in the form of taking money or dispensing brutality) is attested by the fact that all middle-sized and big-city police agencies maintain Internal Affairs Divisions which have as their mission to cope with police corruption. No one needs to know more about the etiology, prevention, and control of police corruption than the police policy-maker and administrator: research information here is of clear practical utility. Second, some police agencies have made considerable progress in developing systematic information on the prevention and detection of police corruption. The New York City Police Department has assembled information systematically on corruption hazards, indicators of corruptive activity, and countermeasures, for example. Despite its twenty-year cycle of scandals and despite the magnitude of the issue there, it is conceivable that New York is as advanced—or more advanced—than any other agency in this respect. Third, only police institutions (albeit with the assistance of a professional researcher) can develop the research information that they need to control police corruption. Good but limited work has been done in advancing the literature, e.g., see Duchane, 1979. But it will only be when police agencies develop the required evaluative information—either through natural or systematic experimentation—that the police can really deal with the problem effectively. Until then, police managers must trust to their own partial experience, intuition, luck, and common sense. That is not all bad, but it could be better.

Developing plans in cooperation with extra-departmental policy-makers and providing leadership to extra-departmental agencies in coordinating the implementation of order-enhancement plans are elements of the new form of police agency. In these activities, no less than in more traditional intradepartmental professional functions, all the attributes of creativity will be required. Without that essential attribute, failure will surely result.

IMPLICATIONS

This chapter has described three features of the new managerial approach, of the new form of police agency. The first is the new partnership between the police agency and the community in order-enhancement plan and policy formulation. The second is a new openness and leadership for the police in working for order enhancement goals. The third, infusing the first two, is a renewed emphasis on creativity. The new managerial approach is the cumulative result of these three emphases.

Efforts to stem crime and disorder in democratic society seem to be failing. By adjusting the form of the primary law enforcement institution from the shape of its mission as it was established in the last century and as it is presently conceived, we can have hope of achieving more acceptable order levels within the context of democracy. This adjustment, built on the new community and new managerial approaches, would require the more effective allocation of police resources—and this can only be done within the context of a new form of police agency.

PART IV

Policy Beginnings

"Any commander who fails to obtain
his objective, and who is not dead or
severely wounded, has not done his full
duty."
PATTON

"Politics is perhaps the only profession
for which no preparation is thought
necessary."
STEVENSON

CHAPTER 8

The Police Manager

How can we begin to develop the new form of police agency, to allocate resources more effectively? Probably we should do just that—begin. Not worrying unduly about the other person, each of the principal actors and the supporting cast should get his or her feet wet—now. The principal actors are the politicians and the police managers; the supporting cast are the criminal justicians—the writers and the educators. "Now" in this context, of course, is a relative term: so let us define it as "whenever the reader finishes this book." The purpose of this section is to offer suggestions for beginning-level approaches for these persons to get their feet wet in the task of working toward this new form of policy agency. The next two chapters suggest Policy Beginnings, respectively, for the police chief and for the politician. Two cautions: others may identify alternative steps more suitable for their own particular locations; and these Policy Beginnings are no more than that—just beginnings.

A CHALLENGE FOR THE CHIEF

Working toward the new form of police agency is a serious challenge for the police chief; fundamental change always brings risks, principally for the tenure of the chief. As a policy beginning, this chapter recommends the incrementalist approach discussed in Chapter 6. Three beginning steps are suggested for the police chief.

First, it is suggested that he establish a "planning-budgeting-resources allocation" system similar to the Manpower Allocation Review System discussed in Chapter 7. The specific design of such a "planning-budgeting-resources allocation" system would be a matter for personal preference, taking into account particular and local circumstances. For fully effective results, however, the design should be systematic, comprehensive, information-supported, analytic, participative, and realistic. The design should involve a recognizable system, one capable of being evaluated, improved, and repeated in subsequent years. The system should be comprehensive in devoting proportional attention to each part of the department, including the quiescent areas giving the manager no immediate problems. If it is not supported by staff analyses in the form of papers for review, the system will be disappointing. Such papers should be analytic, in that options should be identified and quantitative evaluative data utilized. The design should be participative, involving the police chief, the commander of the unit under review, and the principal subordinates of the respective units; the alternative will surely fail. The design should be realistic, planned carefully by a task force so that the entire department will come to understand the intent of the system and so that the details will not be grossly inappropriate. Even so, the first run-through may be disappointing. The area most likely to give difficulties is patrol, and a sound way to approach this is to divide it into several parts by area. The manager should not be deterred, however. Learning from the experience, the system can be improved for better results next time.

Second, the police chief—it is suggested—should make a conscious effort to induce and lead his subordinates in scouring the criminal justice research and other literature for ideas. The intention is that the chief should not fall into the change-for-change's sake trap. Rather, the objective should be to move toward a research basis for operations. A method for achieving this goal is to include this scouring as part of the staff preparation for the "planning-budgeting-resources allocation" cycle.

Third, it is suggested that the police chief look forward to the year when limited participation will be possible in the "planning-budgeting-resources allocation" process by selected extra-departmental personnel. The timing of this addition could well be when the "planning-budgeting-resources allocation" process has become established. The purpose of the intervention would be to begin securing for the police program the benefits of the extra-departmental resources the outsider could bring, as discussed earlier in this publication. A tragedy for the police chief would be to involve a major or other elected official who, for want of ability or preparation, would bring only difficult questions and no additional programmatic support. A tragedy for the community would be a police chief unwilling at an appropriate moment to risk this involvement.

REMAINING CURRENT

A final triple challenge for the police manager is to remain current. The challenge is to him as an individual in continuing to develop his understanding of society and of his craft. It is to him as a departmental leader in ensuring that his subordinates grow in their understanding, and it is to him as a community leader in educating the public in the order-enhancement needs of the community. The basis for this is that he and his department should remain current.

How current are the police chief and his police department? The last decade has produced volumes of operationally significant research on police services. Will these advances be translated into real gains in effectiveness and efficiency, or will they be dissipated in the mere appearance of change, in

uncoordinated and faint improvement activities, and in a
recycling of old "innovations?" The opportunity is available
for a quantum improvement in police field services. As a challenge, this subsection presents data suggestive that police
agencies are currently realizing only marginal realignments.
The data presented are subject to limitations, and they should
be taken with some salt. But the challenge presented by the
data deserves to be taken with the utmost seriousness and
concern.

In the 1981 survey referenced earlier, police agencies
were asked (among many other things) to list major resource
utilization innovations introduced during the past five years
and planned for the coming three years (Farmer, 1981). The
actual questions were—What do you consider to have been
the major innovations introduced in your department in the
utilization of personnel during the past five years for the following functions? What major innovations in the utilization
of personnel do you estimate will be implemented in your
department during the next three years for the following
functions? The "following functions" identified were patrol,
investigations, and traffic. It will be recalled the questions
were asked of U.S. police agencies serving populations greater
than 100,000 and of Virginia police agencies in communities
of more than 5,000 people.

The results of this survey are shown in Tables 4–9. The
first three tables (4–6) summarize the responses from the U.S.
sample of cities with populations greater than 100,000; the last
three tables (7–9) summarize the responses from the Virginia
agencies. Tables 4 and 7 relate to innovations reported as
introduced in patrol; tables 5 and 8 note innovations listed for
the investigative function; and tables 6 and 9 present the
innovations reported as likely to be implemented in the next
three years.

The innovations relating to the radical field service
restructuring opportunity described in Chapter 2 are underlined in each table, as they are of particular interest. Determining which should be listed as so related was somewhat

TABLE 4

Resource Allocation Innovations Reported as Implemented in the
Patrol Function in Police Departments Serving Populations Over
100,000*

Type of innovation	Relative significance index**
Follow-up investigations conducted by patrol officers	1.43
Telephone reporting unit	1.43
Directed patrol (and overtime directed patrol)	10.00
Crime specific sector policing	2.86
Movement to generalist attitude	1.43
Call screening and stacking	2.86
Specific strike force for high-crime areas	1.43
Team policing projects	4.29
Formalized crime analysis capability	8.57
Generalist approach (disbanding several special units)	1.43
Call-back report taking system	1.43
Area sector, beat reporting center concept	1.43
Sector command concept	2.86
Helicopter and horse patrol	2.86
Fixed shifts	7.14
Four-day week	1.43
City divided into 3 patrol precincts	1.43
Weighted beat alignments	1.43
Decentralization	2.86
K–9 Program	6.29
Fleet car plan (each officer has own vehicle)	1.43
Computer models (PECAM, Hypercube)	7.14
Community Service Officer	1.43
Reorganization from 3 platoons to 5	1.43
Unification of patrol and traffic	1.43
One-officer units	2.86
Elimination of walking beats	1.43
Overlapping shifts, longer rotation periods	1.43
New crime reporting systems	2.86
Shifts aligned in smaller squads	1.43
Portable radios	1.43
Higher percentage of police officers on patrol	1.43

TABLE 4 (*continued*)

Type of innovation	Relative significance index**
Tachographs	1.43
Staggered shifts	1.43
Computer aided dispatching	1.43
Manpower-workload assignments ("Power Shift")	5.71
Overtime assignment	1.43

SOURCE: 1981 Police Resources Allocation Survey.
* The items underlined are those which can be considered to be related to the radical field service restructuring opportunity described in Chapter 2. Determining which should be listed as so related should be viewed as somewhat arbitrary because judgment calls were necessarily involved.
**Departments reporting the designated innovations expressed as a percentage of the total number of patrol functions reported.

TABLE 5

Resource Allocation Innovations Reported as Implemented in the Investigative Function in Police Departments Serving Populations Over 100,000*

Type of innovation	Relative significance index**
Managing criminal investigations	10.94
Update of time study	1.57
Plain clothes investigators working with crime analysis information	1.57
Special units for special crime problems	4.69
Case screening/case management; use of solvability factors	14.89
Use of civilian clerks for follow-up investigations	1.57
Follow-up responsibility for certain crimes shifted from patrol to investigative unit	1.57
Telephone response unit	1.57
Career development program	1.57
Specialization in evidence collection	4.69

TABLE 5 (*continued*)

Type of innovation	Relative significance index**
ICAP	3.13
Reassignment of some case follow-up to patrol (especially misdemeanors)	5.71
Decentralization of investigative function	5.71
Total neighborhood team policing	1.57
Telephone follow-up for minor crimes	5.71
Revised case clearance program	1.57
Development of a major crime unit/white collar crime investigative function	1.57
Formation of street crimes unit	1.57
Crime line (anonymous tips taken for reward)	1.57
Crime eye (hidden cameras in businesses)	1.57
Increase in drug buy money	1.57
Airport Narcotics Unit including drug dog	1.57
Use of leased, take-home cars for vice and narcotics personnel	1.57
Flexible "flying squad" for high crime areas	1.57
Computerization of ID section	1.57
Full-time narcotics team	1.57
Sting operation	1.57
Color photography for court evidence	1.57
Crime stopper TV slot	1.57
Victim Witness Coordinator	1.57
Delinquency Prevention Officer	1.57
Recentralization of investigative function	1.57
Beat Zone concept (field sergeants given more latitude in deployment)	1.57
Formalized Crime Analysis	1.57
Crime Specifics Program	1.57
Training in investigative procedures	1.57
Flexie Unit (officers in uniform or plain clothes)	1.57
Manpower assignment based on needs (patterns and trends)	1.57
Computer support	1.57

SOURCE: 1981 Police Resources Allocation Survey.

* The items underlined are those which can be considered to be related to the radical field service restructuring opportunity described in Chapter 2. Determining which should be listed as so related should be viewed as somewhat arbitrary because judgment calls were necessarily involved.

**Department reporting the designated innovation, expressed as a percentage of the total number of investigative innovations reported.

TABLE 6

Resource Allocation Innovations Reported As Future Plans by
Police Departments Serving Populations Over 100,000*

Type of innovation	Relative significance index**
Directed patrol	3.23
MBO	1.08
Training 1st and 2nd level supervisors to assume greater operational responsibility	1.08
Initiation of accountability program	1.08
Taking of officer reports over the phone	2.15
Returning to more generalist officer (rather than specialist)	1.08
Manpower/workload analysis to explore alternative patrol methodologies	1.08
More use of SPSS	1.08
Improved case information data for allocation of investigative personnel	1.08
More sophisticated use of decentralization format	1.08
Improved case screening based on workload, manpower availability, population and crime increases	1.08
Formalized case assignment policy along MCI procedures	1.08
Expand telephone/walk-in report system to include mail-in system	1.08
Computer graphics	1.08
Screening procedure to assign, evaluate, audit case progress	1.08
Call responses alternatives	1.08
Develop more realistic objectives	1.08
Dispatch priority system	1.08
Automated workload analysis of field services	1.08
Alternative Police Response Strategies	2.15
Development of more efficient data system	1.08
Implementation of permanent shifts	2.15
Computer aided dispatch	2.15
Inclusion of investigative and traffic in resource allocation studies	1.08
Automation of information for decision-making	1.08
On-line computer system	2.15

TABLE 6 (*continued*)

Type of innovation	Relative significance index**
Redefinition of beat boundaries	2.15
Automation of officer activity information	1.08
Reinstitution of aviation and special operations section	1.08
Implementation of career development program and restructuring of performance appraisal system	2.15
Use of mini-computer capability	3.23
Reorganization	3.23
Full automation of records	1.08
Improved accounting/resource tracking procedures	1.08
Review of current vehicle procurement/maintenance program	1.08
Long-range planning supported by computer analysis	1.08
Performance budgeting	1.08
Civilianization of some sworn positions	2.15
Use of 4/10 allocation model	1.08
Crime Analysis Unit	3.23
Substation for better allocation of services	1.08
Additional manpower	1.08
Computer patrol car assistance	1.08
Computer monitoring	1.08
Better training for investigators	1.08
Crime Specific Program	1.08
Sector policing	1.08
Crime Prevention Programs	1.08
Community relations	1.08
Evaluate effectiveness of individual programs	1.08
Change from 4 districts to 2	1.08
Detect crime trends; allocate personnel by area, time of day	1.08
Formalization and institutionalization of Operations Analysis	1.08
Change deployment from beat to zone concept	1.08
Conduct thorough review of departmental personnel assignments	1.08
Possible city–county consolidation	1.08
Greater computer use	3.23

TABLE 6 (*continued*)

Type of innovation	Relative significance index**
Formalization of temporal and spatial coding systems for input	1.08
Data Integrity Program	1.08
Computerized management information system	1.08
Restructuring of patrol hours	1.08
Enhanced allocation formula to include Part II crimes	1.08
Emphasis on crime prevention via community participation and awareness	1.08
Improved initial investigations and reporting by uniformed patrol response	1.08
Use of computerized data for ongoing reassessment of patrol activities	1.08
CARD (Computer Aided Resource Deployment)	1.08
Manpower assigned according to demands for service, peak crime hours, etc.	1.08
Increase computer capability for on-line booking, code reporting	1.08
CAD System	1.08
Use of PECAM	2.15
Training of management personnel	1.08
Selective traffic enforcement	1.08
Cost analysis	1.08
Seek new ideas/plans for problems affecting manpower resources (e.g., sick leave abuse, court time, etc.)	1.08

SOURCE: 1981 Police Resources Allocation Survey.

* The items underlined are those which can be considered to be related to the radical field service restructuring opportunity described in Chapter 2. Determining which should be listed as so related should be viewed as somewhat arbitrary because judgment calls were necessarily involved.

**Departments reporting the designated innovation expressed as a percentage of the total number of innovations planned for future implementation.

arbitrary, as judgment was involved in estimating the nature of the innovation in the mind of the respondent; others may have made other classification judgments. In parentheses it should be noted that any change described as an innovation by a respondent has been so listed. Some readers may consider some of the innovations as quite noninnovative. But that is

TABLE 7
Resource Allocation Innovations Reported as Implemented in the Patrol Function in Police Departments in Virginia Serving Populations of 5,000–100,000*

Type of innovation	Relative significance index**
Follow-up investigations conducted by patrol officers	10
Directed patrol	10
Crime specific sector policing	10
Development of Services Division	10
Realigning Criminal Investigations Unit	10
Reorganization from 3 platoons to 5	10
One-officer units	10
Platoon system of scheduling	10
Manpower-workload assignments ("Power Shift")	20

SOURCE: 1981 Police Resources Allocation Survey.
* The items underlined are those which can be considered to be related to the radical field service restructuring opportunity described in Chapter 2. Determining which should be listed as so related should be viewed as somewhat arbitrary because judgment calls were necessarily involved.
**Departments reporting the designated innovations expressed as a percentage of the total number of patrol functions reported.

TABLE 8
Resource Allocation Innovations Reported as Implemented in the Investigative Function in Police Departments in Virginia Serving Populations of 5,000–100,000*

Type of innovation	Relative significance index**
Reassignment of some case follow-up to patrol (especially misdemeanors)	16.67
Decentralization of investigative function	16.67
Directed patrol	16.67
Recentralization of investigative function	33.32
Development of improved resource allocation model	16.67

SOURCE: 1981 Police Resources Allocation Survey.
* The items underlined are those which can be considered to be related to the radical field service restructuring opportunity described in Chapter 2. Determining which should be listed as so related should be viewed as somewhat arbitrary because judgment calls were necessarily involved.
**Departments reporting the designated innovations expressed as a percentage of the total number of investigative functions reported.

TABLE 9

Resource Allocation Innovations Reported as Future Plans by
Police Departments in Virginia Serving Populations of 5,000–
100,000*

Type of innovation	Relative significance index**
Directed patrol	9.09
ICAP	9.09
Police Support Officer Program	9.09
Implementation of career development program and restructuring of performance appraisal system	9.09
Review of current vehicle procurement/ maintenance program	9.09
Greater computer use	27.27
Emphasis on crime prevention via community participation and awareness	18.18
Ongoing training for officers	9.09

SOURCE: 1981 Police Resources Allocation Survey.
* The items underlined are those which can be considered to be related to the radical field service restructuring opportunity described in Chapter 2. Determining which should be listed as so related should be viewed as somewhat arbitrary because judgment calls were necessarily involved.
**Departments reporting the designated innovations expressed as a percentage of the total number of innovations planned for future implementation.

really beside the point: the listings are of innovations as defined by the respondents.

The substantial limitations of the data, as indications of the state-of-reform in the use of police resources, should be stressed. First, a mail questionnaire was used, and open-ended questions were utilized in gathering this particular set of information. Clearly on-site interviews would have produced better information. They would have facilitated the development of a "positive" attitude by the respondents, and would have removed the "inhibitions" for respondents asked to write down items. Even though this questionnaire was accompanied by a letter of endorsement from the Police Executive Research Forum, the use of open-ended questions cannot be expected to have produced completely full responses. Second, a study specifically designed to ask questions about changes in field operations would have asked more—and more probing—questions. Such a study would have also made appropriate use of other information sources on the topic, e.g., the results of other studies on administrative and programmatic changes in policing. In sum, the present data should be viewed as presenting only a partial view of the situation.

Three major comments are suggested by the data. These concern the evidence relating to the extent of a coordinated restructuring of police field services, evidence relating to the level of innovation in police management, and evidence relating to the need for more information on the subject.

There is little evidence in the data of a vast and coordinated restructuring of the entire range of police field services activity. There is evidence of change being effected throughout the range. For example, a long list of changes in the investigative function will be noted. But the changes listed seem marginal; they do not seem conceived as a radical reformulation of the character of police service. If he could see any of the departments after the changes had been implemented, O. W. Wilson (it may be guessed) would not be astounded.

Nor would O. W. be astonished at the level of creativity or novelty in the innovations. Without exception, the changes proposed seem relatively pedestrian—many reappearing from the past. Horse patrol has been a change utilized in a number of cities, for example; but it is difficult to think of this change as an innovation.

Henry Thoreau commented that "Some circumstantial evidence is very strong, as when you find a trout in the milk" (Thoreau, 1918). The evidence is different here, because these data show the absence of a trout. Whether this lack of coordinated restructuring and of creative innovation is a function of the data collection methodology or of reality is open to question. Certainly, the absence of evidence is not necessarily evidence of the absence of either coordinated restructuring or of creativity in innovation. But it is suggestive. The data alert the police manager to pay attention to the issue.

CHAPTER 9

The Elected Official

It may be difficult for some to understand why politicians should be permitted a more significant role in police policy-making and evaluation. A basic reason is that such involvement is the only way that the kind of order-enhancement program "that will do the job" can be mounted and executed in a community. On the debit side—of the occupational groups that have earned the public's mistrust, politicians are considered by many surely to deserve it the most. For these the term "politician" is little more than a dirty word. In dealing with crime control and police matters a great many politicians certainly have acted shamefully and contrary to the public interest; a great many have behaved as if reelection were their primary or only moral imperative; a great many have proven misinformed; so many have been corrupt. Much of the history of American policing has been the struggle to throw off the confining and corruptive shackles of "bad politics." Capping this, the power of the politician is relatively so great that—even if the entire breed were saints—Jefferson, Acton, and the rest of us would have good reason to distrust them.

Outweighing the risks are four realities. The politician, the right politician, does have "power" to make available to the police institution—the power, for example, of ensuring the coordination and cooperation of other governmental and nongovernmetal units in working toward order-enhancement goals. The right politician has the capability to facilitate an opening up of the police bureaucracy. The alternative to good politics is not no politics but bad politics. The right politician has the specific duty of making policy and of evaluating programs, as elementary civics texts explain. But the word "politician" has sunk so low in public estimation that hesitation to trust is natural.

The right politician is here taken as the official elected with primary responsibility for the police function. In most cities, this is the mayor. In some, it can be a single council member or a committee. In the states, it is usually the governor. This chapter is addressed primarily to these elected officials: for convenience, we will call them collectively the "mayor." But other politicians may also see in this an appropriate role for themselves.

CHALLENGE FOR THE ELECTED OFFICIAL

As a beginning for effective policy involvement, it is suggested that the mayor take three steps.

The first is to begin acquiring the sound information base that a politician needs in order to discharge leadership responsibility in the police and criminal justice areas. The effective political leader, in this area as in others, needs more than skill at politics; required also is sufficient technical understanding of the substantive area of police and criminal justice policy-making and management. The mayor needs to know enough to be able not only to understand issues raised by the police manager but also to be able to give policy leadership both to the police agency and to the community.

Acquiring an adequate knowledge base should be a matter of reading, listening, and looking. For reading, the elected official should turn to the basic textbooks of policing and criminal justice in order to gain a systematic picture of the area. For listening and for a listing of suitable books, the elected official should establish contact with the criminal justice or similar program in the nearest university. It is precisely because the university is an excellent source of "ivory tower" thinking that the practical politician needs it. He already has the practical advice of his police and similar agencies, the practical considerations of his fellow politicians, and knowledge of the practical realities of his own political environment. The ivory tower, while not providing "the answer," can offer a real help for the politician drowning in practicality. And not all the information from the ivory tower will be impractical.

For those politicians with the time and the commitment, there really is no alternative to looking—looking at their own police and criminal justice institutions. Armed with the intellectual framework that the reading and listening can provide, this looking will surely pay off in practical ideas for improvement. For the police agency, the method is simple. Ride with police officers; tell them that you are there, not to help, but to look and learn; ride with more police officers on all three shifts, on hectic Friday evenings and on quiet Sunday mornings; talk with all the commanders; look at their records; ride with more patrol officers. Be prepared to hear much that is foolish and some that is insulting to the intelligence—but much will also be heard that is perceptive and to-the-point. The best location for finding out about a police department is in a squad car. In the office, there is a tendency for the officer to give out the official myth; as a rule of thumb, in a squad car every third officer will tell it like it is. They will do so after they become convinced that the listener cares, that he is discreet, and that he understands.

The second step is to work to make available the technical and financial resources required for the police institution and for the community to undertake the planning and evaluation activities that are needed. The resources required can be expected to be small but critical. The police institution may require technical assistance, perhaps from qualified consultants, in establishing a "planning-budgeting-resources allocation" system. The city council, or equivalent body, would need technical and staff assistance in participating in the planning and evaluation activities noted earlier. The other governmental agencies and private organizations would require stimulation and help in working with the police institution in developing order-enhancement plans.

The claim that the police agency has insufficient resources to introduce new activities like planning and evaluation should be recognized as likely to be a red herring, and this underscores the need for the politician to have a sound information base. Without this information base the mayor is defenseless against this claim: he is in no position to know. While on this issue, it should be added that there is no magic formula for calculating the number of officers required per 1,000 population, comparing the ratio in the communities with those in others in the same population group. The only sound way of determining the number required is through a "planning-budgeting-resources allocation" process that begins by determining specific goals and calculates the manpower resources required to achieve such goals.

The third step is to develop a strategy for encouraging the police institution to take the lead in effecting the required initiatives for change, for exerting the influences described in Chapter 4. The shape of this strategy would depend on local circumstances. But such a plan is likely to have at least three components. There would be some stock-taking of the local situation—of the needs, obstacles, and opportunities. There would be a need for some catalytic event. In some communities this could be achieved by narrowing the responsibility of the police agency (e.g., by providing for exclusion of the police from traffic regulation activity, as Norval Morris suggested), for example; in others it could be achieved by replacing the police chief and by civilianizing the principal police positions. And there would be a need for continuing public education.

No one would suggest that such steps would be either easy or enough. They are no more than suggestions for Policy Beginning.

NO NOVELTY

The view that police agencies are policy-making bodies and that politicians should become involved in the policy-setting is not at all new to the criminal justice literature. This deserves reemphasis.

Chapter 1 noted Kenneth Culp Davis' view that what is needed is to confine, check, and structure discretion. Providing the reemphasis, let us report his prescription more fully. In addition to effective supervision and appeals, he advocated open plans, open policy statements, open findings, open reasons, open rules, open precedents, and fair informal procedures. His corrective program for the police specified ten actions. Educate the public that police make policy. Redefine crime so that laws do not overshoot. Specify police powers and keep police to them. Close the gap between police manuals and the activities of police behavior. Raise policy-making from the officer to chief. Bring policy-making out into the open. Invite public comment. Harmonize with the democratic principle. Study the situation, and eliminate ad hoc officer discretion.

KNOWLEDGE BASE

It is quite possible to direct a public agency without any more than the most general knowledge of the functional area—the tragedy is that many politicians and some police managers do just this. But the politician without an adequate knowledge base cannot seriously expect to provide the political leadership that is really needed. The politician serious about controlling crime must first arm himself by becoming familiar with the fundamentals of the criminal justice "body of knowledge," with the basic facts and with the best thinking on the subject. The politician serious enough about criminal justice to be reading this book must be viewed as having started step 1 of the Policy Beginning—that of acquiring an adequate information base. This subsection is intended to facilitate that process by suggesting additional reading.

For this purpose, the field is divided (artificially) into seven segments—criminal justice system, jurisprudence, law enforcement, corrections, courts, criminal justice research, and criminology and crime prevention. Two lists are offered. The first suggests one book from each segment; the second, in Appendix A, lists a number of publications under each of the headings. A caveat and an apology must at the same time be entered. The caveat is that these lists omit much that is excellent. The apology is to the authors whose works are excluded, because so much else in the literature is indeed excellent.

The elected official who reads, and thinks through the local implications of, the books on the shorter list will have a basic grasp of the subject. He will know the basic dimensions of the body of knowledge.

1. *On the Criminal Justice System*—Silberman, Charles, *Criminal Justice, Criminal Violence*, New York: Randam House (1978).
2. *On Jurisprudence*—Pound, Roscoe, *An Introduction to the Philosophy of Law*, New Haven: Yale University Press (1954).
3. *On Law Enforcement*—Wilson, O. W. and Roy McLaren, *Police Administration*, New York: McGraw-Hill (1977).
4. *On Corrections*—Keve, Paul W., *Prison Life and Human Worth*, Minneapolis: Minneapolis Press (1974).
5. *On Courts*—Neubauer, David W., *America's Courts and the Criminal Justice System*, N. Scituate, Massachusetts: Duxbury Press (1979).
6. *On Criminal Justice Research*—Morris, Norval and Michael Tonry, *An Annual Review of Research*, Vols 1, 2,

3, 4, or 5, Chicago: The University of Chicago Press (1979, 1980, and subsequently).

7. *On Criminology and Crime Prevention*—Nettler, Gwynn, *Explaining Crime*, New York: McGraw-Hill (1974).

The politician would do well to heed the biblical exhortation to find wisdom: "Wisdom is the principal thing; therefore get wisdom: and with all thy getting, get understanding" (Proverbs 4:7).

CHAPTER 10

Epilogue

So commonplace has crime become that many tend to be fatalistic about it, accepting it as "natural and normal" for contemporary society and feeling that nothing really can be done about it. Many read horrific accounts of gross criminal violations as if they were tales from a distant land, not real events happening in our own real world and threatening us and our way of life. Many are pessimistic about opportunities for coping with the situation.

The message of this book is different. Crime can be controlled to the extent that communities make more appropriate use of their police resources. Needed is a new form of police agency. Chapter 1 pointed out that, without working toward such a new form, communities will continue to misuse their police resources. Chapter 2 described studies showing how police resources should be redirected. Chapter 3 pointed out the difficulties of the administrator in moving toward goals, and provided an example of failure—of how resources allocation has focused on process, rather than ends. Chapter 4 discussed the political context of policing, demonstrated the insufficiency of the "professional model," and showed how police agencies can learn to use the forces of the political process. Three realities of police–political relations were urged. Communities must accept that politics permeates policing; that police decision-making can be improved not by denying but by recognizing and manipulating the political element; and that, while some are bad, certain political intrusions are desirable. Chapter 5, in discussion of the purposes of policing, offered a socio-economic view of the function of policing. Chapter 6 described the new community approach required of communities and elected officials wishing the open type of police institution that is needed. It emphasized the need to place a profit-making burden on the police administrator and to insist on receptivity to new modes of thought. Chapter 7 gave an account of the new managerial approach that is required from police administrators. It discussed the key characteristics of the new form of police agency—the kind of planning, openness, and creativity that are required if society is to realize its crime control dreams. The final two chapters made suggestions for communities wishing to begin: Chapter 8 addressed the police manager, and Chapter 9 the politician. In so doing, this book has given an account of two administrative entities. Police resources allocation decision-making was analyzed, and recommendations were offered for an improved approach. The contemporary police institution was also described; the characteristics needed for the new form of police agency were discussed.

Both social science considerations and personal impression convince that fatalism—the fatalism about crime referenced in the first paragraph—is misplaced. From the social science perspective, we have drawn critical facts, interpretations and inferences—variously—from an information base consisting of nationwide and other survey research data on police agency practice, from the application of microeconomic tools to the police situation, from criminal justice research studies, and from criminal justice and related literatures. Using this base, this publication has broken new ground, particularly in enlarging understanding of police resources allocation decision-making and in suggesting a radical reconceptualization of the process. Using this base, it has been argued that a new form of police agency, with more effective utilization of personnel, is necessary for adequate crime control. This has been fleshed out, it is true, by adding advisory information in Chapters 8 and 9 suggested by a management consulting framework, and by describing a limited planning-budgeting-resource allocation system with which the writer was involved in the reality-context of a large police agency. Nevertheless, the conclusions of this work are grounded in what can be characterized as social science considerations. The considerations give reasonable confidence that we have the capability and the information to effect the changes that are needed to cope.

From the perspective of personal impression, it has long seemed to the writer that our police officers are ill-served by their police institutions, that the officers are better at their function than the supporting-agency is at its function. These impressions are based on working with all ranks of police officers, all sizes of police departments, and all shapes of local governments throughout the nation. These have included some fifty jurisdictions, ranging from the smallest to the largest and from the East to the West Coast. It is impossible to spend years with an occupational group without developing strong feelings of attachment, without in this case—as it were—growing a badge. Certainly, some police personnel are corrupt and vicious, many are limited human beings—the range in work ability that is present in any occupation is also present here. Certainly, the average educational level holds back the development of professionalism. But, all said and done, a good cop—one who is streetwise, decent, intelligent, and solid—is a joy to behold. He or she can be a master craftsman, playing the hideous and crazy reality of the street with an elegance not unlike a skilled musician playing a violin. The same cannot be said for police agencies. While there are fine police chiefs and police commanders, the full development of a fine police agency remains for the future. The officers deserve more from their agencies.

How long must we wait for implementation of the new form of police agency, for the improved allocation of police resources? This is hard to say. On the one hand, the time required for implementation of new techniques in public agencies can be considerable, and experiences such as the Dark Ages are testimony to the substantial capacity of human groups to absorb tragedy and punishment. Further, it will deter some that the change is not a panacea: even after its implementation, we will be left with the other considerable obstacles to order enhancement that are outside the police agency, such as the condition of the laws and of the rest of the criminal justice system. On the other hand, this publication does indicate that we have the capability and the information to begin the changes now; and every year lost in waiting serves only to perpetuate the suffering of individuals and the risk to society. The new form of police agency can give us the beginning we want in addressing our crime problems. We need not wait; we should not delay. We should be able to enjoy the policing we deserve.

References

Abney, G., and T. P. Lauth (1979). "City Council Intervention in Police Administration," Meyer, Fred A., and Ralph Baker (eds.), *Determinants of Law Enforcement Policies*, Lexington, Massachusetts: Lexington Books.

American Bar Association (1974). *Economics of Crime and Corrections: Bibliography*, Washington, D.C.: American Bar Association.

American Justice Institute (1974). *Project STAR (System and Training Analysis of Requirements)—Police Officer Role Training Program*, Sacramento, California: California Commission on Police Officer Standards and Training.

Anderson, R. W. (1976). *Economics of Crime*, London, England: Macmillan Press.

Austin, S. (1978). "Crime as Employment; What a Way to Make a Living," Leon Leiburg (ed.), *Crime and Employment Issues: A Collection of Policy-Relevant Monographs*, Washington, D.C.: American University.

Azzi, C., and R. Ehrenberg (1975). "Household Allocation of Time and Church Attendance," *Journal of Political Economy*, Vol. 83, February 1975.

Baer, R. K. (1979). "Labor Market Determinants of Male Crime Rates," *Proceedings of Criminal Justice Statistics Association*, Washington, D.C.: Criminal Justice Statistics Association.

Bammi, Deepak (1972). *Design of Police Patrol Beats to Minimize Response Time to Calls for Service*, Ph.D. Thesis, Chicago, Illinois: Illinois Institute of Technology.

Barnard, Chester (1938). *The Functions of the Chief Executive*, Cambridge, Massachusetts: Harvard University Press.

Baumol, William J. (1959). *Business Behavior, Value and Growth*, New York, New York: Harcourt, Brace and World.

Becker, Gary (1968). "Crime and Punishment: An Economic Approach," *Journal of Political Economy*, March–April 1968.

Becker, Gary (1973). "A Theory of Marriage," *Journal of Political Economy*, Vol. 81, No. 4, July–August 1973.

Becker, Gary (1976). *The Economic Approach to Human Behavior*, Chicago, Illinois: University of Chicago Press.

Beecher, J. A., R. L. Lineberry, and M. J. Rich (1981). "Politics of Police Responses to Urban Crime," Lewis, Dan A. (ed.), *Reactions to Crime*, Beverly Hills, California: Sage Publications, Inc.

Benson, Walter R. (1970). *Systems Analysis of Criminalistics Operations*, Kansas City, Missouri: Midwest Research Institute.

Bergstrom, Theodore C., and R. P. Goodman (1973). "Private Demand for Public Goods," *The American Economic Review*, June 1973.

Bieck, William and Kansas City Police Department (1977). *Response Time Analysis (Summary; Vol. I Methodology; Vol. II Analysis)*, Kansas City, Missouri: Kansas City Police Department.

Bieck, William and Kansas City Police Department (1979). *Response Time Analysis (Vol. III, Part II Crime Analysis)*, Kansas City, Missouri: Kansas City Police Department.

Bieck, William and Kansas City Police Department (1980). *Response Time Analysis (Vol. IV, Non-Crime Call Analysis; Synopsis)*, Kansas City, Missouri: Kansas City Police Department.

Bittner, Egon (1975). "Capacity to Use Force as the Core of the Police Role," Skolnick, Jerome H., and Thomas C. Gray (eds.), *Police in America*, Boston, Massachusetts: Little Brown.

Block, Peter B., and James Bell (1976). *Managing Investigations: The Rochester System*, Washington, D.C.: Police Foundation.

Borcherding, Thomas E., and R. T. Deacon (1972). "The Demand for the Services of Non-Federal Governments," *The American Economic Review*, December 1972.

Bottoms, Albert H. (1969). *Allocation of Resources in the Chicago Police Department*, Chicago, Illinois: City of Chicago Police Department.

Bottoms, Albert H., and Ernest K. Nilsson (1970). "Operations Research," *Police Chief*, May 1970.

Bowers, N. (1975). *Crime, Punishment and the Mode of Production: An Exploratory Study*, Ph.D. dissertation, Columbia, Missouri: University of Missouri.

Boyle, R. F. (1979). "Should Politics Play a Role in Police Administration?" Schultz, Donald O., (ed.), *Modern Police Administration*, Houston, Texas: Gulf Publishing Company.

Breton, Albert (1974). *The Economic Theory of Representative Government*, Chicago, Illinois, Aldine Publishing Company.

Breton, Albert (1978). *The Economic Constitution of Federal States*, Toronto, Canada: University of Toronto Press.

Bright, J. A. (1969). *Beat Patrol Experiment*, London, England: Home Office.

Brown, M. E. (1979). "Economic Correlates of Female Criminality," *Proceedings of Criminal Justice Statistics Association*, Washington, D.C.: Criminal Justice Statistics Association.

Buchanan, James M. (1967). *The Demand and Supply of Public Goods*, Chicago, Illinois: Rand McNally and Company.

Buckner, T., and N. Christie (1974). "Police and Culture," Szabo, D. (ed.), *Police Culture and Society*, Montreal, Canada: University of Montreal Press.

Bunyan, T. (1976). *Political Police in Britain: History and Practice*, New York, New York: St. Martin's Press.

Cahn, Michael F., and James M. Tien (1981). *An Evaluation Report of an Alternative Approach in Police Response: The Wilmington Management of Demand Program*, Cambridge, Massachusetts: Public Systems Evaluation, Inc.

Center for Research on Criminal Justice (1977). *Iron Fist and the Velvet Glove: An Analysis of the U.S. Police*, Berkeley, California: Center for Research on Criminal Justice.

Chaiken, Jan M. (1974). *The Impact of Police Activity on the Crime of Robbery in the New York City Subway System*, New York, New York: Rand Corporation.

Chaiken, Jan M. (1975). *Patrol Allocation Methodology for Police Departments*, Washington, D.C.: H.U.D.

Chaiken, Jan M., and Peter Dormant (1975). *Patrol Car Allocation Model: Executive Summary*, Washington, D.C.: H.U.D.. Also *Patrol*

Car Allocation Model: User's Manual, Washington, D.C.: H.U.D. and *Patrol Car Allocation Model: Program Description*, Washington, D.C.: H.U.D.

Chaiken, Jan M., T. Crabill, L. Holliday, D. Jaquette, M. Lawless, and E. Quade (1976). *Criminal Justice Models: An Overview*, Washington, D.C.: G.P.O.

Chambliss, W. J. (1971). "Vice, Corruption, Bureaucracy and Power," *Wisconsin Law Review*, 1971, No. 4, pp. 1150–1173.

Chamelin, N. C. (1978). "Role of Law Enforcement and Police Protection," Apostolik, Elinid (ed.), *Legislative Issues in Crime Control*, Athens, Georgia: University of Georgia Institute of Government.

Chapman, Samuel (ed.), (1970). *Police Patrol Readings*. Springfield, Illinois: Charles C. Thomas.

Cloninger, D. O. (1975). *Economics of Crime and Law Enforcement*, Sarasota, Florida: Omni-Print Incorporated.

Cole, G. F. (1980). *Criminal Justice: Law and Politics*, 3rd Edition, Belmont, California: Wadsworth Corporation.

Conrad, Robert F. (1980). *Modeling the Short-Run Behavior of the Hospital Industry using a Joint Cost Function*, unpublished paper, Durham, North Carolina: Department of Economics, Duke University.

Cunningham, William C., and Todd Taylor (1984). Crime and Protection in America: A Study of Private Security and Law Enforcement Resources and Relationships, McLean, Virginia: Hallcrest Systems; unpublished report.

Darrough, M. N., and J. M. Heinecke (1978). "The Multi-Output Translog Production Cost Function: The Case of Law Enforcement Agencies," J. M. Heinecke (ed.), *Economic Models of Criminal Behavior*, Amsterdam: North-Holland Publishing.

Davis, Edward M., and L. Knowles (1975). "A Critique of the Report: An Evaluation of the Kansas City Preventive Patrol Experiment," *Police Chief*, Vol. XLII, No. 6.

Davis, Kenneth Culp (1971). *Discretionary Justice: A Preliminary Inquiry*, Urbanna, Illinois: University of Illinois Press.

DeAlessi, Louis (1969). "Implications of Property Rights for Government Investment of Choices," *American Economic Review*, Vol. 59, March 1969.

Decotiis, T. A., and T. A. Kochan (1978). "Professionalization and Unions in Law Enforcement," Cromwell, Paul F., and George

Keefer (eds.), *Police Community Relations: Selected Readings,* St. Paul, Minnesota: West Publishing Company.

Downs, Anthony (1967). *Inside Bureaucracy,* Santa Monica, California: Rand Corporation.

Duchane, Nina (1979). *The Literature of Police Corruption, Volume II: A Selected, Annotated Bibliography,* New York, New York: The John Jay Press.

Eck, John (1979). *Burglary Investigation Decision Model Replication,* Washington, D.C.: Police Executive Research Forum.

Eck, John E. (1983). *Solving Crimes: The Investigation of Burglary and Robbery,* Washington, D.C.: Police Executive Research Forum.

Ehrlich, I. (1975). "Capital Punishment: A Case of Life or Death," *American Economic Review,* June 1975.

Emerson, Robert D. (1972). *An Economic Analysis of the Provision of Police Services,* Ph.D. Thesis, Lafayette, Indiana: Purdue University.

Eskridge, C. W. (1978). *Economics of Criminal Justice Bibliography,* Washington, D.C.: G.P.O.

Farmer, David J. (1976). "Fact Versus Fact: A Selective View of Police Research in the United States," *The Police Journal,* Vol. XLIX, April–June.

Farmer, David J. (1978). "The Research Revolution," *Police Magazine,* Reprinted in *Target Magazine,* January 1979.

Farmer, David J. (1980). "Out of Hugger-Mugger: The Case of Police Field Services," Clarke, Ronald, and Michael Hough (eds.), *Police Effectiveness,* Lexington, Massachusetts: Lexington Press.

Farmer, David J. (1981). "Police Resources Allocation Survey," Richmond, Virginia: Virginia Commonwealth University.

Farmer, David J. (1981). "Thinking About Research: The Contribution of Social Science Research to Contemporary Policing," *Police Studies,* Vol. 3, No. 4.

Farmer, David J. (1982). "Police Resources Allocation: Toward a Theory," *Police Studies,* Vol. 5, No. 2.

Farmer, David J. (1983). "Manpower Allocation in the New York City Police Department," London, England: University of London.

Farmer, Michael T. (1981). *Differential Police Response Strategies,* Washington, D.C.: Police Executive Research Forum.

Feinberg, S. E., K. Larntz, and Al Reiss (1976). "Redesigning the Kansas City Preventive Patrol Experiment," *Evaluation,* Vol. 3, Nos. 1–2.

Feraud, H. (1977). "Police and the Prevention of Crime," Third Criminological Colloquium, Council of Europe, Strasbourg, France, July 1977.

Ferrara, J. (1975). *Comparing Methods of Allocating Patrol Units,* Cambridge, Massachusetts: Massachusetts Institute of Technology.

Feville, P., and H. A. Juris (1976). "Police Professionalization and Police Unions," *Sociology of Work and Occupations,* Vol. 3, No. 1.

Fischer-Kowalski, M., F. Leitner, and H. Steinert (1976). "Status Management and Interactional Conflict of the Police," *International Journal of Criminology and Penology,* Vol. 4, No. 2, New York, New York: Academic Press Incorporated.

Fisk, J. G. (1973). Discussion Paper About Some Dimensions of Police Discretion, Los Angeles, California: University of California, Los Angeles Institute of Government and Public Affairs.

Fogelson, Robert M. (1977). *Big-City Police,* Cambridge, Massachusetts: Harvard University Press.

Gabor, I. R., and C. Low (1975). "Police Role in the Community," Curran, James T., and Richard H. Ward (eds.), *Police and Law Enforcement,* Volume 2, New York, New York: AMS Press, Inc.

Getz, Malcolm (1979). *The Economics of the Urban Fire Department,* Baltimore, Maryland: John Hopkins University Press.

Getz, Malcolm (1980). *Public Libraries: An Economic View,* Baltimore, Maryland: John Hopkins University Press.

Giertz, I. Fred (1970). *An Economic Analysis of the Distribution of Police Patrol Forces,* Washington, D.C.: National Institute of Law Enforcement and Criminal Justice.

Georgia State Crime Commission (1977). *Correlation Analysis of Criminal Justice and Demographic Variables in Georgia,* Washington, D.C.: G.P.O.

Goldstein, Herman (1977). *Policing a Free Society,* Cambridge, Massachusetts: Ballinger Publishing Company.

Goldstein, Herman (1979). "Improving Policing: Problem-Oriented Policing," *Crime and Delinquency,* Vol. 25, No. 2.

Greenberg, Bernard, Oliver S. Yu, and Karen I. Lang (1973). *Enhancement of the Investigative Function, Volume IV: Burglary Investigative Checklist and Handbook,* Springfield, Virginia: National Technical Information Service.

Greenberg, Bernard, Carola V. Elliott, Lois P. Kraft, and H. Steven Proctor, (1977). *Felony Investigation Decision Model: An Analysis of Investigative Elements of Information,* Washington, D.C.: G.P.O.

Greenblatt, S. L. (1980). *Boston in the Post-World War 2 Period: Latent Political Conflict Becomes Blatant*, Evanton, Illinois: Northwestern University Center for Urban Affairs and Policy Research.

Greenwood, Peter, Jan Chaiken, and Joan Petersilia (1976). *The Criminal Investigation Process*, Santa Monica, California: Rand Corporation.

Grimmond, Jo (1978). "Introductory Remarks," Seldon, Arthur (ed.), *The Economics of Politics*, Lancing, West Sussex: The Institute of Economic Affairs.

Haller, M. H. (1970). "Urban Crime and Criminal Justice: The Chicago Case," *Journal of American History*, Vol. 57, No. 3.

Hammermesh, D., and N. M. Soss (1974). "An Economic Theory of Suicide," *Journal of Political Economy*, Vol. 82, January–February 1974.

Hanewicz, W. B., and T. R. Minick (1981). "Comprehensive Law Enforcement Planning Network: Borrowing from Another Public Service," Lagoy, Stephen (ed.), *New Perspectives on Urban Crime*, Jonesboro, Tennessee: Pilgrimage Press.

Harris, K. D. (1980). *Crime and the Environment*, Springfield, Illinois: Charles C. Thomas.

Hauser, N. *et al.* (1969). *Computer Simulation of a Police Emergency Response System*, Polytechnic Institute of Brooklyn Report PB-211-311, National Technical Information Service, Washington, D.C.: U.S. Department of Commerce.

Heinecke, J. M. (1978). *Supply of Legal and Illegal Activity*, Stanford, California: Center for Econometric Studies of the Justice System, Stanford University.

Hellman, D. A. (1979). *Urban Police Sector and Urban Crime—A Simultaneous System Approach*, Washington, D.C.: G.P.O.

Hicks, J. R. (1946). *Value and Capital*, New York, New York: Oxford University Press.

Hilton, J. (1972). "Police, Politics and Young People," *Police Journal*, Volume 45, No. 1.

Hoover Institution (1978). *Property Crime and the Returns to Legitimate and Illegitimate Activities*, Stanford, California: Center for Econometric Studies of the Justice System, Stanford University.

Jakubs, D. L. (1977). "Police Violence in Time of Political Tension: The Case of Brazil," Bayley, David H. (ed.), *Police and Society*, Beverly Hills, California: Sage Publications.

Johnson, B. C. (1976). "Taking Care of Labor: The Police in American Politics," *Theory and Society*, Vol. 3, No. 1.

Johnson, T. A. (1972). "Police-Citizen Encounters and the Importance of Role Conceptualization for Police Community Relations," *Issues in Criminology*, Vol. 7, No. 1.

Kakalik, J., and S. Wildhorn (1971). *Private Police in the United States*, Vol. 1: Findings and Recommendations; Vol. 2: The Private Police Industry: Its Nature and Extent; R-869-DOJ; Santa Monica, California: Rand Corporation.

Kakalik, James S., and S. Wildhorn (1971). *Aids to Decision-Making in Police Patrol*, Washington, D.C.: H.U.D.

Kakalik, James S., and S. Wildhorn (1971). *The Private Police: Security and Danger*, Washington, D.C.: G.P.O.

Katz, M. (1974). "Violence and Civility in a Suburban Milieu," *Journal of Police Science and Administration*, Vol. 2, No. 3.

Keller, R. L. (1975). "American Police: Minority or Political Subculture," Kenton, Jack (ed.), *Police Roles in the Seventies: Professionalism in America*, Aurora, Illinois: Social Service and Sociological Resources.

Kelling, George L., Tony Pate, Duane Dieckman, and Charles E. Brown (1974). *The Kansas City Preventive Patrol Experiment: A Technical Report*, Washington, D.C.: Police Foundation.

Knight, R. (1977). "Police Role in Our Permissive Society," *International Criminal Police Review*, Vol. 32, No. 310.

Knight, R. C. (1982). "Police and Politics: Political Control," *Australian Police Journal*, Volume 36, No. 2.

Kolesar, Peter, K. Ricter, T. Crabill, and W. Walker (1974). *A Queuing-Linear Programming Approach to Scheduling Police Patrol Cars*, New York, New York: The New York City Rand Institute.

Kolesar, Peter, and W. E. Walker (1975). *A Simulation Model of Police Patrol Operations: Executive Summary*, Washington, D.C.: H.U.D.. Also *A Simulation Model of Police Patrol Operations: Program Description*, Washington, D.C.: H.U.D.

Landes, W. M. (1974). "An Economic Analysis of the Courts," Landes, W. M. and Gary Becker (eds.), *Essays in the Economics of Crime and Punishment*, New York, New York: Columbia University Press.

Lantier, J. (1970). *Le Temps des Policiers: Trente Ans d'Abus*, Paris, France: Librairie Arthème Fayard.

Larson, Richard C. (1972). *Urban Police Patrol Analysis*, Cambridge, Massachusetts: M.I.T. Press.

Larson, Richard C. (1975). *Hypercube Queuing Model: Program Description*, Washington, D.C.: H.U.D.

Larson, Richard (1975). "What Happened to Patrol Operations in Kansas City? A Review of the Kansas City Preventive Patrol Experiment," *Journal of Criminal Justice*, Vol. 3, No. 4.

Lautmann, R. (1971). "Political Sovereignty and Police Compulsion," Lautmann, R. and J. Feest (eds.), *Police-Sociological Studies and Reports on Research*, Opladen, West Germany: Westdeutscher Verlag GMBH.

Lawson, P. E. (1981). "Mediation of Social Order: Police Use of Law, Myth and Mystifications," *Police Studies*, Vol. 4, No. 2.

Leiter, Robert O., and Gerald Sirkin (1979). *Economics of Public Choice.* New York, New York: Cyco Press Incorporation.

Lindblom, Charles E. (1959). "The Science of Muddling Through," *Public Administration Review*, Vol. 9, No. 2.

Lipset, S. M. (1974). "Why Cops Hate Liberals—and Vice Versa," Goldsmith, Jack and Sharon S. Goldsmith (eds.), *Police Community: Dimensions of an Occupational Subculture*, Pacific Palisades, California: Palisades Publishers.

Lowi, Theodore J. (1969). *The End of Liberalism*, New York, New York: W. W. Norton.

Machlup, Fritz (1967). "Theories of the Firm: Marginalist, Behavioral, Managerial," *American Economic Review*, Vol. 57, March 1967.

Manning, Peter K. (1978). *Policing: A View From the Street*, Santa Monica, California: Goodyear Publishing Company.

Marris, R. (1964). *The Economic Theory of Managerial Capitalism*, New York, New York: Free Press.

Marschak, J. (1965). "Economics of Language," *Behavioral Science*, Vol. 10, April 1965.

Massachusetts Legislative Research Council (1965). *Report Relative to State Police Promotions*, Boston, Massachusetts: Massachusetts Legislative Research Council.

McEwen, Thomas (1966). *Allocation of Police Manpower Resources in the St. Louis Police Department*, Vols. I and II, St. Louis, Missouri: St. Louis Police Department.

McEwen, Thomas (1968). *A Mathematical Model for Prediction of Police Patrol, Resource Allocation Project*, St. Louis, Missouri: St. Louis Police Department.

McEwen, Thomas, and Richard C. Larson (1974). "Patrol Planning in the Rotterdam Police Department," *Journal of Criminal Justice*, Vol. 2, No. 1.

McNamara, Joseph D. (1974). "Preface," Kelling, George L., Tony Pate, Duane Dieckman and Charles E. Brown, *The Kansas City Preventive Patrol Experiment: A Technical Report*, Washington, D.C.: Police Foundation.

McPheters, Lee R., and W. B. Stronge (1974). "Law Enforcement Expenditures and Urban Crime," *National Tax Journal*, Vol. 27, No. 4, December 1974.

McPheters, Lee R., and William B. Stronge (1976). *The Economics of Crime and Law Enforcement*, Springfield, Illinois: C. Thomas.

Meadows, R. J., "Perspectives for Change: Expanding the Police Role in Crime Prevention," *Police Chief* **46**, 4, International Association of Chiefs of Police, April 1979.

Migue, J. L., and C. Belanger (1974). "Toward A General Theory of Managerial Discretion," *Public Choice*, Vol. 17, Spring 1974.

Miller, W. R. (1977). "Never on Sunday: Moralistic Reformers and the Police in London and New York City, 1830–1870," Bayley, David H. (ed.), *Police and Society*, Beverly Hills, California: Sage Publications.

Moore, M. D. (1978). "Police In Search of Direction," Gaines, Larry and Truett A. Ricks (eds.), *Managing the Police Organization: Selected Readings*, St. Paul, Minnesota: West Publishing Company.

Morgan, D. R. and C. Swanson (1976). "Analyzing Police Policies: The Impact of Environment, Politics and Crime," *Urban Affairs Quarterly*, Vol. II, No. 4.

Morrow, William L. (1980). *Public Administration: Politics and the Political System*, New York, New York: Random House.

Mudge, Richard (1974). *A Description of the New York City Police Department RMP Allocation Model*, New York, New York: The New York City Rand Institute, unpublished.

Murphy, Patrick V. (1977). *Commissioner: A View from the Top of American Law Enforcement*, New York, New York: Simon and Shuster.

Naisbitt, John (1982). *Megatrends: Ten New Directions Transforming Our Lives*, New York, New York: Warner Books, Inc.

National Advisory Commission on Criminal Justice Standards and Goals (1976). *Report of the Task Force on Private Security*, Washington, D.C.: G.P.O.

National Institute of Law Enforcement and Criminal Justice (1977). *The Criminal Investigation Process: A Dialogue on Research Findings*, Washington, D.C.: G.P.O.

Niskanen, W. A. (1971). *Bureaucracy and Representative Government,* Chicago, Illinois: Aldine-Artherton.

N.Y.P.D. (1972). "MARS Package," unpublished, New York, New York: New York City Police Department.

O'Brien, J. T. (1978). "Chief and the Executive: Direction or Political Interference?" *Journal of Police Science and Administration,* Vol. 6, No. 4.

O'Neill, N. W. (1974). *Role of the Police: Normative Role Expectations in a Metropolitan Police Department,* unpublished dissertation, State University of New York at Albany.

Orzechowski, William (1977). "Economic Models of Bureaucracy: Survey, Extensions, and Evidence," Borcherding, Thomas (ed.), *Budgets and Bureaucrats: The Sources of Government Growth,* Durham, North Carolina: Duke University Press.

Parker, Brian, and Joseph Peterson (1972). *Physical Evidence Utilization in the Administration of Justice,* Berkeley, California: University of California at Berkeley.

Parker, Brian, and Vonnie Gurgin (1972). *The Role of Criminalistics in the World of the Future,* Menlo Park, California: Stanford Research Institute.

Parkinson, C. Northcote (1957). *Parkinson's Law and Other Studies in Administration,* Boston, Massachusetts: Houghton Mifflin.

Pate, Tony (1976). *Police Response Time: Its Determinants and Effects,* Washington, D.C.: Police Foundation.

Peterson, Joseph (1974). *Utilization of Criminalistic Services by the Police: An Analysis of the Physical Evidence Recovery Process,* Washington, D. C.: G.P.O.

Peterson, Joseph (1979). *Crime Laboratory Proficiency Study,* Washington, D.C.: G.P.O.

Phillips, Llad (1978). "Factor Demand in the Provision of Public Safety," J. M. Heinecke (ed.), *Economic Models of Criminal Behavior,* Amsterdam: North-Holland.

Pogue, Thomas E. (1975). "Effect of Police Expenditures on Crime Rates: Some Evidence," *Public Finance Quarterly,* Vol. 3, No. 1.

Poole, R. W. (1973). *Crime and Demographic Profile,* Washington, D.C.: U.S. Department of Justice.

Posner, R. (1973). *Economic Analysis of Law,* Boston, Massachusetts: Little Brown.

President's Commission on Crime in the District of Columbia (1966).

Report of the President's Commission on Crime in the District of Columbia, Washington, D.C.: G.P.O.

President's Commission on Law Enforcement and Administration of Justice (1967). *The Challenge of Crime in a Free Society*, Washington, D.C.: G.P.O.

Press, S. J. (1971). *Some Effects of an Increase in Police Manpower in the 20th Precinct of New York City*, New York, New York: Rand Institute.

Public Administration Service (1969). *Police Services in the City of New Hope, Minnesota*, Chicago, Illinois: Public Administration Service.

Purdy, E. W. (1978). Unpublished Paper presented at Special National Workshop on Forensic Science Services and the Administration of Justice, Kenner, Louisiana.

Reiner, R. (1981). "Politics of Police Powers," Adlam, Diana (ed.), *Politics and Power Four*, Boston, Massachusetts: Routledge and Kegan Paul.

Reinier, Hobart (1976). *NEP Crime Analysis: Site Visit Report*, Bloomington, Indiana: Foundation for Research and Development in Law Enforcement and Criminal Justice.

Reinier, Hobart G. (1977). *Crime Analysis in Support of Patrol*, Washington, D.C.: G.P.O.

Reith, Charles (1952). *The Blind Eye of History: A Study of the Origins of the Present Police Era*, Reprinted 1975, Montclair, New Jersey: Patterson Smith.

Remington, Frank (1980). "The Police: An Important Substantive Policy-Making Agency of Government," Foust, Cleon H., and D. Robert Webster (eds.), *An Anatomy of Criminal Justice*, Lexington, Massachusetts: Lexington Books.

Rivlin, Alice (1972). *Systematic Thinking for Social Action*, Washington, D.C.: Brookings Institute.

Robbins, Lionel (1962). *An Essay on the Nature and Significance of Economic Science*, London: MacMillan and Company.

Roby, P. A. (1974). "Politics and Prostitution: A Case Study of the Revision, Enforcement, and Administration of the New York State Penal Laws on Prostitution," Susman, J. (ed.), *Crime and Justice: An AMS Anthology*, New York, New York: AMS Press Incorporated.

Rosenthal, P., and D. A. Travnicek (1974). *Analysis of Criminalistics Laboratory Effectiveness in Criminal Justice Systems*, Washington, D.C.: Calspan Corporation.

Rottenberg, S. (1973). *Economics of Crime and Punishment*, Conference of the American Enterprise Institute for Public Policy Research, Washington, D.C.: American Enterprise Institute.

Rubinstein, Jonathan (1973). *City Police*, New York, New York: Farrar, Straus and Giroux.

Rumbaut, R. G., and Egon Bittner (1979). "Changing Conceptions of the Police Role: A Sociological Review," Morris, Norval, and Michael Tonry (eds.), *Crime and Justice: An Annual Review of Research*, Vol. I, Chicago, Illinois: University of Chicago Press.

Saladin, Booke A. (1980). A Methodology for the Allocation of Police Patrol Vehicles, Ph.D. Thesis, Columbus, Ohio: Ohio State University.

Samuelson, Paul (1951). *Economics*, New York, New York, McGraw-Hill.

Schell, Theodore, *et al.* (1976). *Traditional Preventive Patrol, N.E.P. Phase I Summary Report*, Washington, D.C.: G.P.O.

Schnelle, J. F., *et al.* (1977). "Patrol Evaluation Research: A Multiple-Baseline Analysis of Saturation Police Patrolling During Day and Night Hours," *Journal of Applied Behavior Analysis*, Vol. 10.

Scitovsky, Tibor (1943). "A Note on Profit Maximization and Its Implication," *Review of Economic Studies* Vol. XI, pp. 57–60.

Sedgewick, J. L. (1978). *Welfare Economics and Criminal Justice Policy*, Ph.D. Dissertation, Charlottesville, Virginia: University of Virginia.

Seidman, D., and M. Couzens (1974). "Getting the Crime Rate Down: Political Pressure and Crime Reporting," *Law and Society Review*, Vol. 8, No. 3.

Sharkansky, Ira (1975). *Public Administration: Policy Making in Government Agencies*, Chicago, Illinois: Rand McNally.

Shearing, C. D., and J. S. Leon (1977). "Reconsidering the Police Role: A Challenge to a Challenge of a Popular Conception," *Canadian Journal of Criminology and Corrections*, Vol. 19, No. 14.

Shumate, R. P., and R. F. Crowther (1966). "Quantitative Methods for Optimizing the Allocation of Police Resources," *Journal of Criminal Law, Criminology and Political Science*, Vol. 57, pp. 197–206.

Silberman, Charles E. (1978). *Criminal Violence, Criminal Justice*, New York, New York: Random House.

Simon, Herbert A. (1945). *Administrative Behavior: A Study of Decision-Making Processes in Administrative Organization*, New York, New York: Macmillan.

Simon, Herbert A. (1959). "Theories of Decision-Making in Economics and Behavioral Science," *American Economic Review*, June 1959.

Smith, S. B., and Deepak Bammi (1973). *Superbeat: A System for the Effective Distribution of Police Patrol Units*, Chicago, Illinois: Illinois Institute of Technology.

Smith, V. (1975). "The Primitive Hunter Culture, Pleistocene Extinction, and the Rise of Agriculture," *Journal of Political Economy*, Vol. 83, August 1975.

Solicitor-General of Canada (1971). "Police Function in Our Changing Society," *Proceedings of Conference "A"—the Role of the Policeman*, Lake Couchiching, Ontario; Ottawa, Ontario: Canadian Solicitor General.

Spelman, William, and Dale K. Brown (1981). *Calling the Police: Citizen Reporting of Serious Crime*, Washington, D.C.: Police Executive Research Forum.

Stead, Philip John (1981). "The Nature of Police Command," The Thirteenth Frank Newsam Memorial Lecture, *Police Studies*, Vol. IV, No. 1.

Stigler, George (1970). "The Optimum Enforcement of Laws," *Journal of Police Economy*, May–June 1970.

Straver, M. A. (1979). "Difference Between Doctrine and Reality: How Can It Be Cured?" *Deviance et Society*, Vol. 3, No. 4.

Sullivan, R. F. (1973). "Economics of Crime—An Introduction to the Literature," *Crime and Delinquency*, Vol. 19, No. 2.

Summers, Anita *et al.* (1977). "Do Schools Make a Difference?" *American Economic Review*, Vol. 67, September 1977.

Summers, Anita *et al.* (1979). *Improving the Use of Empirical Research as a Policy Tool: An Application to Education*, Discussion paper, pp. 579–580, Madison, Wisconsin: University of Wisconsin Press.

Teaseley, C. E. (1978). "Police Role Perceptions: Their Operationalization and Some Preliminary Findings," *Criminal Justice Review*, Vol. 3, No. 1, Atlanta, Georgia: Georgia State University School of Urban Life.

Thoreau, Henry David (1918). Unpublished manuscript in *Miscellanies, Biographical Sketch*, Vol. X, p. 30.

Tien, James M., James W. Simon, and Richard C. Larsen (1979). *An Alternative Approach in Police Patrol: The Wilmington Split-Force Experiment*, Cambridge, Massachusetts: Public Systems Evaluation.

Tien, James M., and Michael Cahn (1980). "Management of Demand: A Productivity-Oriented Approach to Meeting the Demand for Public Services," I.E.E.E. Conference on Systems, Man and Cybernetics, Cambridge, Massachusetts, October 1980.

Toffler, Alvin (1980). *The Third Wave*, New York, New York: William Morrow and Company.

Truman, David B. (1951). *The Governmental Process*, New York, New York: Alfred A. Knopf.

Tullock, C. (1969). "An Economic Approach to Crime," *Social Science Quarterly*, June 1969.

Tullock, Gordon (1965). *The Politics of Bureaucracy*, Washington, D.C.: Public Affairs Press.

U.C.L.A. (1974). *An Analysis of the Los Angeles Police Department's Patrol Car Deployment Methods*, Los Angeles, California: Engineering School Report, UCLA.

Urban Sciences (1971). *Computer Simulation of the Boston Police Department*, Wellesley, Massachusetts: Urban Sciences.

Urban Sciences (1972). *Police Resources Allocation Program (RAP)*, Wellesley, Massachusetts: Urban Sciences.

Van Mises, L. (1944). *Bureaucracy*, New Haven, Connecticut: Yale University Press.

Viteritti, J. P. (1973). *Police, Politics and Pluralism in New York City: A Comparative Case Study*, Beverly Hills, California: Sage Publications.

Walder, S. (1976). "Police Professionalism: Another Look at the Issues," *Journal of Sociology and Social Welfare*, Volume 3, No. 6.

Walton, Frank (1970). "Selective Distribution of Police Patrol Force," Chapman, Samuel C. (ed.), *Police Patrol Readings*, Springfield, Illinois: Charles C. Thomas.

Walzer, Norman (1972). "Economics of Scale and Municipal Police Services: The Illinois Experience," *Review of Economics and Statistics*, November 1972.

Ward, Richard H. (1971). The Investigative Function: Criminal Investigation in the United States, University of California at Berkeley, unpublished dissertation.

Ward, Richard H. (1975). "Police Role: A Case of Diversity," Coffey, Alan R., and Vernon E. Renner (eds.), *Criminal Justice as a System: Readings*, Englewood Cliffs, New Jersey: Prentice-Hall.

White, S. O. (1974). "Perspectives on Police Professionalization," Goldsmith, Jack, and Sharon S. Goldsmith (eds.), *Police Commu-*

nity: Dimensions of an Occupational Subculture, Pacific Palisades, California: Palisades Publishers.

Wickersham Commission (1931). "Report on the Police," *Report of the National Commission on Law Observance and Enforcement*, Vol. 14, Washington, D.C.: G.P.O.

Williamson, Oliver E. (1964). *The Economics of Discretionary Behavior: Managerial Objectives in a Theory of the Firm*, Englewood Cliffs, New Jersey: Prentice-Hall.

Wilson, James Q. (1963). "Police and Their Problems: A Theory," *Public Policy*, Vol. 12.

Wilson, James Q. (1968). *Varieties of Police Behavior*, Cambridge, Massachusetts: Harvard University Press.

Wilson, James Q. (1972). "Politics and the Police," in Cole, G. F. (ed.), *Criminal Justice: Law and Politics*, Belmont, California: Wadsworth Publishing Company.

Wilson, James Q. (1975). *Thinking About Crime*, New York, New York: Basic Books.

Wilson, James Q., and B. Boland (1978). "The Effects of the Police on Crime," *Law and Society Review*, Vol. 12.

Wilson, Orlando W. (1941). *Distribution of Police Patrol Force*, Publication 74, Chicago, Illinois: Public Administration Service.

Wilson, Orlando W., and Roy McLaren (1978). *Police Administration*, New York, New York: McGraw-Hill.

Witte, Anne (1980). *Economics of Public Service Delivery Systems*, Special National Workshop on Research Methodology and Criminal Justice Evaluation, unpublished paper, Baltimore, Maryland: National Institute of Justice.

Zimring, Frank E. (1976). "Field Experiments in General Deterrence: Preferring the Tortoise to the Hare," *Evaluation*, Vol. 3, Nos. 1–2.

APPENDIX

Reading List for the Elected Official

This reading list is intended for elected officials wishing to acquire a sound knowledge base for exercising leadership in achieving crime control results in their jurisdictions. Chapter 9 discussed this policy beginning. This reading list is, of course, broader than the earlier list of references in that it covers a wider range of criminal justice issues.

CRIMINAL JUSTICE SYSTEM

Bowker, Lee H. *Women and Crime in America*, New York: Macmillan (1981).

Chang, Dae. *Criminology: A Cross-Cultural Perspective*, Durham, NC: Carolina Academic Press (1976).

Duffee, David, Frederick Hussey, and John Kramer. *Criminal Justice: Organization, Structure and Analysis*, Englewood Cliffs, NJ: Prentice-Hall, Inc. (1978).

McNeely, R. L., and Carl Pope, eds. *Race, Crime and Criminal Justice*, Beverly Hills, CA: Sage Publications (1981).

Radzinowicz, Sir Leon, and Marvin Wolfgang. *Crime and Justice* (Vol. I, *Criminal in Society*; Vol. II, *Criminal in the Arms of the Law*; Vol. III, *Criminal under Restraint*) New York: Basic Books (1977).

Shelley, Louis. *Readings in Comparative Criminology*. Carbondale, IL: Southern Illinois University Press (1981).

Silberman, Charles. *Criminal Justice, Criminal Violence*. New York: Random House (1978).

Price, Barbara Raffel, and Natalie Sokoloff, eds. *The Criminal Justice System and Women*. New York: Clark Boardman Co. (1982).

National Advisory Commission on Civil Disorders (Kerner Commission). Washington, D.C.: Government Printing Office (1968).

National Advisory Commission on Criminal Justice Standards and Goals. Washington, D.C.: Government Printing Office (1973).
   -A National Strategy to Reduce Crime
   -Police
   -Courts
   -Corrections
   -Community Crime Prevention
   -Proceedings on the National Conference on Criminal Justice

President's Commission on Law Enforcement and Administration and Justice. Washington, D.C.: Government Printing Office (1967).
   -Crime and Its Impact
   -Police
   -Courts
   -Corrections
   -Drunkenness
   -Juvenile Delinquency and Youth Crime
   -Narcotics and Drug Abuse
   -Organized Crime
   -Science and Technology

JURISPRUDENCE

Cohen, Morris R. and Felix S., eds. *Readings in Jurisprudence and Legal Philosophy*. Englewood Cliffs, NJ: Prentice-Hall Inc. (1951).

Duster, Troy. *The Legislation of Morality: Law, Drugs and Moral Judgment*. New York: The Free Press (1970).

Ehrlich, E. *Fundamental Principles of the Sociology of Law*. Cambridge: Harvard University Press (1936).

Friedman, Lawrence M. *A History of American Law*. New York: Simon and Schuster (1973).

Friedman, Lawrence, and S. Macaulay, eds. *Law and the Behavioral Sciences*. Indianapolis: Bobbs-Merrill Co. (1969).

Hoebel, E. *The Law of Primitive Man.* Cambridge: Harvard University Press (1961).

Llewellyn, K. and E. Hoebel. *The Cheyenne Way: Conflict and Case Law in Primitive Jurisprudence.* Tulsa: University of Oklahoma Press (1941).

Merryman, John H. *The Civil Law Tradition.* Stanford, CA: Stanford University Press (1969).

Pound, Roscoe. *An Introduction to the Philosophy of Law.* New Haven: Yale University Press (1954).

Reasons, Charles E. and Robert M. Rich, eds. *The Sociology of Law: A Conflict Perspective.* Toronto: Butterworths (1978).

Schur, Edwin M. *Law and Society: A Sociological View.* New York: Random House (1968).

Schwartz, R., and J. Skolnick, eds. *Society and the Legal Order.* New York: Basic Books (1970).

Simon, Rita James, ed. *The Sociology of Law: Interdisciplinary Readings.* Scranton, PA: Chandler Publishing Co. (1968).

Skolnick, Jerome H. *Justice Without Trial.* New York: John Wiley and Sons (1966).

Smigel, Erwin O. *The Wall Street Lawyer.* New York: Free Press (1964).

Stark, Rodney. *Police Riots.* Belmont, CA: Wadsworth (1972).

LAW ENFORCEMENT

Clarke, Ronald *et al. Police Effectiveness.* Lexington, MA: Lexington Books (1980).

Fogelson, Robert. *Big-City Police.* Cambridge, MA: Harvard University Press (1977).

Garmire, Bernard L. *Local Government Police Management,* 2nd ed. Washington, D.C.: International City Management Association, (1982).

Geary, David. *Community Relations and the Administration of Justice.* New York: John Wiley and Sons (1975).

Goldstein, Herman. *Police in a Free Society.* Cambridge: Ballinger Press (1977).

Horne, Peter. *Women in Law Enforcement.* Springfield, IL: Charles C. Thomas Publications (1975).

Iannone, N. F. *Supervision of Police Personnel,* 3rd ed. Englewood Cliffs, NJ: Prentice-Hall Inc. (1980).

Niederhoffer, Arthur. *Behind the Shield.* Garden City, NY: Doubleday
   & Co., Inc. (1967).
Niederhoffer, Arthur, and Abraham S. Blumberg. *The Ambivalent
   Force,* 2nd ed. Hillsdale, IL: The Dryden Press (1976).
Reppetto, Thomas. *The Blue Parade.* New York: Free Press (1978).
Rubenstein, Jonathan. *City Police.* New York: Farrar, Straus & Giroux
   (1973).
Staufenberger, Richard. *Progress in Policing.* Cambridge, MA: Ballinger
   Press (1980).
Wilson, James Q. *Varieties of Police Behavior.* Cambridge, MA: Harvard
   University Press (1978).
Wilson, O. W., and Roy Clinton McLaren. *Police Administration,* 4th
   ed.. New York: McGraw-Hill Book Co. (1977).

CORRECTIONS

Bowker, Lee H. *Corrections: The Science and the Art.* New York: Mac-
   millan (1982).
Carter, Robert M., Daniel Glaser, and Leslie T. Wilkins. *Correctional
   Institutions.* New York: J. B. Lippincott Co. (1977).
Freeman, John, ed. *Prisons Past and Future.* Exeter, NH: Heinemann
   (1978).
Galaway, Burt, and Joe Hudson. *Offender Restitution in Theory and
   Action.* Lexington, MA: Lexington Books (1978).
Goldfarb, Ronald. *Jails: The Ultimate Ghetto.* Garden City, NY: Anchor
   Press (1975).
Jacobs, James B. *Stateville: The Penitentiary in Mass Society.* Chicago:
   University of Chicago Press (1977).
Keve, Paul W. *Corrections.* New York: John Wiley & Sons (1981).
Keve, Paul W. *Prison Life and Human Worth.* Minneapolis, MN: Uni-
   versity of Minnesota Press (1974).
Lockwood, Daniel. *Prison Sexual Violence.* New York: Elsevier (1980).
McGee, Richard A. *Prisons and Politics.* Lexington, MA: Lexington
   Books (1981).
Mennel, Robert M. *Thorns and Thistles.* Hanover, NH: University Press
   of New England (1973).
Menninger, Karl. *The Crime of Imprisonment.* New York: Viking Press
   (1966).

Morris, Norval. *The Future of Imprisonment*. Chicago: University of Chicago Press (1974).

Rothman, David. *Conscience and Convenience*. Boston: Little, Brown and Co. (1980).

————. *The Discovery of the Asylum*. Boston: Little, Brown and Co. (1971).

Smykla, John Ortiz. *Community-Based Corrections: Principles and Practices*. New York: Macmillan (1981).

Sykes, Gresham M. *The Society of Captives*. Princeton: Princeton University Press (1958).

Ward, David A., and Kenneth F. Schoen. *Confinement in Maximum Custody*. Lexington, MA: Lexington Books (1981).

COURTS

ABA Standards Relating to the Administration of Criminal Justice. Washington, D.C.: ABA Criminal Justice Section (1978).

The Criminal Law Revolution and its Aftermath, 6th ed.. Washington, D.C.: Bureau of National Affairs (1978).

The Criminal Law Revolution and its Aftermath, 1977–1980 Supplement. Washington, D.C.: Bureau of National Affairs (1981).

Fair and Certain Punishment: Report of the Twentieth Century Fund Task Force on Criminal Sentencing. New York: McGraw Hill (1976).

Frankel, Marvin E. *Criminal Sentences: Law Without Order*. New York: Hill and Wang (1973).

Kittrie, Nicholas N. *The Right to be Different*. Baltimore: Penguin (1971).

Klein, Irving J. *Constitutional Law for Criminal Justice Professionals*. N. Scituate, MA: Duxbury Press (1980).

LaFave, Wayne R. and A. W. Scott. *Handbook on Criminal Law*. St. Paul, MN: West Publishers (1972).

McCarthy, F. B. and J. G. Carr. *Juvenile Law and its Process*. Charlottesville, VA: Bobbs-Merrill (1980).

Neubauer, David W. *America's Courts and the Criminal Justice System*. N. Scituate, MA: Duxbury Press (1979).

Uniform Rules of Criminal Procedure: Comparison and Analysis. Washington, D.C.: ABA Criminal Justice Section (1978).

Zeisel, Hans. *Bail Revisited*. Chicago: American Bar Foundation (1979).

CRIMINAL JUSTICE RESEARCH

Conley, John A. ed. *Theory and Research in Criminal Justice: Current Perspectives*. Cincinnati: Anderson Publishing Co. (1979).

Erikson, Kai T. *Wayward Puritans: A Study in the Sociology of Deviance*. New York: John Wiley and Sons (1966).

Hagan, Frank E. *Research Methods in Criminal Justice and Criminology*. New York: Macmillan (1982).

Johnson, Edwin S. *Research Methods in Criminology and Criminal Justice*. Englewood Cliffs, NJ: Prentice-Hall Inc. (1981).

Morris, Norval and Michael Tonry. *Crime and Justice: An Annual Review of Research*. Vols. 1, 2, 3, 4, or 5, Chicago: The University of Chicago Press, (1979, 1980, and subsequently).

Palmer, Ted. *Correctional Intervention and Research*. Lexington, MA: Lexington Books (1978).

Talarico, Susette M., ed. *Criminal Justice Research: Approaches, Problems, and Policy*. Cincinnati: Anderson Publishing Co. (1980).

CRIMINOLOGY AND CRIME PREVENTION

Akers, Ronald, and Richard Hawkins, eds. *Law and Control in Society*. Englewood Cliffs, NJ: Prentice-Hall, Inc. (1975).

Beccaria, C. *On Crimes and Punishment*. Translated by Henry Paducci. Indianapolis: The Bobbs-Merrill Company (1975).

Empey, LaMar T. *American Delinquency*. Homewood, IL: The Dorsey Press (1978).

Jacoby, Joseph E., ed. *Classics of Criminology*. Oak Park, IL: Moore Publishing Company (1979).

Long, Elton, et al. *American Minorities: The Justice Issue*. Englewood Cliffs, NJ: Prentice-Hall, Inc. (1975).

Nettler, Gwynn. *Explaining Crime*. New York: McGraw-Hill Book Co. (1974).

Stevenson, Leslie. *Seven Theories of Human Nature*. New York: Oxford University Press (1974).

Taylor, Ian, et al. *Critical Criminology*. Boston: Routledge & Kegan Paul (1975).

Turk, Austin T. *Criminality and Legal Order*. Chicago: Rand McNally and Company (1969).

Jeffrey, C. Ray. *Crime Prevention Through Environmental Design.* Beverly Hills, CA: Sage Publications (1977).

National Institute for Juvenile Justice and Delinquency Prevention. *Preventing Delinquency (Vol. 1): A Comparative Analysis of Delinquency Prevention Theory.* Washington, D.C.: U.S. Department of Justice (1977).

Newman, Oscar. *Design Guidelines for Creating Defensible Space.* Washington, D.C.: National Institute of Law Enforcement and Criminal Justice (1977).

Index

227